Dear R
Best of ×
in medical

The Glowing Reviews Profit System

One-Page Blueprint to Generate
More Reviews and Increase
Revenue for Your Small Business

Jennifer Sun

Table of Contents

Introduction

You may have noticed the significant effect of the pandemic on businesses and organizations. Consumers now trust other people more than your company, thus the popularity of online reviews. People now rely on other customers' feedback to decide where to buy.

As an entrepreneur, you can't avoid online reviews. Your customers will likely find your company online regardless of your business type, and they often check your reviews first before transacting with you. Therefore, your online reputation is everything.

If your business generates more positive reviews, your brand becomes trustworthy. You'll gain more customers, but what happens if you have a single bad review? It can dwarf the excellent feedback from your other clients.

The 2021 Podium State of Online Reviews reported that 81% of consumers wouldn't buy from businesses with less than a 3-star rating (Baer, 2021). Therefore, it's only fitting that you feel worried about your business. But worrying will get you nowhere. You should take action.

I understand your dilemma, and it's the reason I wrote this book. The R.E.V.I.E.W. method can be your catalyst in discovering how to turn things around and generate more revenues. Let me discuss this technique further.

What Is the R.E.V.I.E.W. Method?

R.E.V.I.E.W. is an acronym for *Research, Engage, Value, Improve, Engage,* and *Win*. It is the one-page blueprint that forms the foundation of this book. We'll refer to it as we go along. But first, let's discuss each one briefly.

- *Research*: You should know your customers and what they need.

- *Engage*: You must communicate with your clients and offer exceptional service.

- *Value*: As a business owner, you can provide incentives for customers who leave honest reviews.

- *Improve*: You can only be successful if you continuously refine your products and services based on customer feedback.

- *Engage*: Make it a point to reply to positive and negative reviews. But always remember to be professional.

- *Win*: If you can satisfy your customers, they can become brand advocates.

This R.E.V.I.E.W. method will guide you as we discuss the 10 core steps you need for your business to thrive. But you may be curious about the benefits of reading my book. I'll cite them next.

Benefits You'll Gain From Reading
The Glowing Reviews Profit System

Now that you have this book, prepare to learn five things.

Proven Strategies

First, you can now access practical, proven strategies to gain more revenues and positive reviews for your small business. Apply them and see the improvement in customer trust and online reputation.

Time-Saving Techniques

Second, I'll share my expertise and experience with you on how you can save time and effort efficiently. Then, learn to implement these effective review generation methods. If you do, you'll have more time to focus on the pressing needs of the business.

Enhanced Customer Satisfaction

Third, you'll also learn how to boost customer service and satisfaction. Doing so gains customer loyalty, repeat business, and positive reviews.

Competitive Advantage

Fourth, you'll gain a competitive advantage by attracting more customers. You can achieve a better online reputation using the techniques and strategies I shared in this book.

Long-Term Business Growth

Lastly, you can achieve sustainable growth if you implement the techniques in this book. Moreover, you'll gain a more substantial market presence and increased revenue.

Aside from taking advantage of the benefits, wouldn't it be nice to learn shortcuts to achieve your financial goals faster?

Shortcuts You'll Gain From The Glowing Reviews Profit System

When you read this book, you'll learn the following shortcuts:

Streamlined Frameworks

First, you'll find the signature frameworks easy to understand and follow. Therefore, you can quickly use the review generation techniques without starting from scratch.

Expert Guidance

Second, I'll share my extensive experience to help you avoid prevalent barriers and risks. My tried-and-tested methodologies can guide you to success.

Prioritized Action Steps

Third, you don't have to run in circles because this book can help you focus on strategies offering the best impact. I help ensure the effective and efficient investment of your time and resources.

Customizable Solutions

Fourth, I'll provide several frameworks you can tailor to fit your needs. Therefore, you can quickly implement the right strategies for your specific situation.

Ongoing Improvement

Lastly, you'll realize you need continuous learning and adaptation to beat your competitors. Learning from this book allows you to adjust your game plan to achieve lasting success.

There is no overnight success. Before writing this book, I had to go through ups and downs. It took years of experience to accumulate knowledge, and I now share my learnings with you.

Building an online reputation can be challenging. Even celebrities experienced some blows to their reputation. For instance, Robert Downey Jr. had his share of challenges with cycles of drug addiction and rehab. He's a great actor, but no one took him seriously. However, look at how Robert Downey Jr. changed himself. He's been sober for several years, and people love him as their Iron Man.

Recently, *The Fast and the Furious* star Vin Diesel is now a social media celebrity with at least 93 million Instagram followers. His posts consist of happenings with his family. So why do people love him? He's authentic.

What can we learn about reputation management from these two celebrities? First, consumers want authenticity and transparency from the business they patronize. If your company has these qualities, these buyers will reward you. Thus, manage your reputation by handling your business's public image. How? Let this book teach you.

What You'll Learn From The Glowing Reviews Profit System

You'll hit the ground running with this book. Use the time-tested techniques and strategies I'll share to receive positive reviews continuously. Build an online reputation and continually improve it to enjoy your clients' trust and loyalty.

As you boost your reputation, you will, in turn, notice a significant increase in your business revenue. You'll continue to generate repeat business from satisfied customers. More importantly, they will tell others to patronize your business. As a result, your revenue growth will finally open more expansion opportunities. Moreover, it will offer financial stability.

The newfound expertise and knowledge you learn from this book will help you manage your online presence. You can devise ways to maintain customer satisfaction and outperform your competitors. Learn how to outpace your competition in this dynamic digital environment.

Lastly, reap the benefits of your successful and thriving business with the strategies and skills I shared. Achieve your business and professional goals, and build a lasting image in your industry or community. As your company thrives, you'll have more resources and time for other pursuits, leading to a balanced and more fulfilled life.

You may have had a hard time keeping your business afloat because of a single bad online review you had from an unsatisfied client. You can finally recover from this experience with the new learnings you'll gain from this book. Use the techniques and strategies wisely if you want a successful business.

We've been talking about reputation management and reviews. Do you know how important these concepts are? The following section will help you.

Chapter 1:

The Importance of Reviews and Reputation Management

You don't build a business. You build people, and people build the business. –Zig Ziglar

Reviews are vital for social proof, SEO enhancement, and building brand trust. Thus, if you actively seek reviews, you get crucial feedback for business growth. Reputation management helps you maintain a positive online presence and ensure customer retention.

You should grasp the significance of reviews and reputation management to boost revenue. But first, let's talk about why customer feedback matters to your business.

Why Reviews Matter: Social Proof, SEO, and Brand Trustworthiness

The internet has revolutionized how people buy and use products and services. Digital reviews have become critical to decision-making. Thus, it's vital to comprehend why customer feedback matters to your business.

Why Are Online Reviews Significant for Your Business?

Online reviews have become essential to purchasing. Before visiting a business, 90% of buyers consult these reviews (Chan, 2023).

Unfortunately, negative reviews also play a vital role. Because of negative reviews, 94% of online shoppers decide not to patronize a particular shop (ReviewTrackers, 2022a).

For any business, having a robust online presence is crucial, and customer reviews play a vital role in achieving this. They enhance the customer experience and create a positive online image. This section will discuss why customer reviews are crucial to your brand.

Customer Reviews Boost Your Company's Online Visibility

First, getting customer reviews is essential for boosting your online visibility. Search engines value positive customer feedback. Thus, your business can rank higher if it has good reviews. Also, it can result in your recognition as a field expert, and you enjoy increased visibility online.

Customer Reviews Help Build Your Business's Credibility

Second, customer reviews build your brand's credibility, which can lead to more views, website traffic, and sales. Thus, strive to have a positive reputation for creating awareness among customers.

Customer Reviews Make Your Website Rank on Search Engines

Third, customer reviews can generate significant online exposure for your business. Search engines like Google favor highly rated companies with review velocity. They use user feedback from popular review sites. Thus, if you have high ratings in reviews, you have a higher chance of being at the top of the Google search results.

Consequently, positive reviews can attract more customers, generating more reviews. As you gain more reviews, more satisfied clients will likely share their experiences about your business.

Customer Reviews Increase Your Bottom Line

Fourth, positive customer reviews can affect a business's financial performance. A study by Harvard Business School revealed the correlation between reviews and economic success. According to the research, positive ratings on Yelp.com can cause a 5–9% increase in sales in the short term (Luca, 2016). Thus, even minor improvements can create a considerable effect.

Customer Reviews Allow You to Connect With Consumers

Fifth, customer reviews provide an excellent opportunity to connect with customers. By responding to positive and negative feedback, you can create a friendly and welcoming image of your brand. As a result, it can help increase visibility and promote the business. MedQuest, for example, has seen a substantial increase in Facebook and Google reviews by engaging with their customers (Reputation, n.d.).

Customer Reviews Attract New Clients

Sixth, positive customer reviews can be very effective in increasing sales. Seriously Silly Socks, for example, offers a discount voucher to customers who leave a review (Willas, 2023). By doing so, the company raised its sales and attracted new buyers. Also, offering customers incentives for feedback can help establish trust and social proof.

What Is Social Proof?

Social proof involves people seeking guidance from others. Advertisers have used the concept for years. With the internet and social media, the importance of social proof has grown.

Customer reviews and shared experiences can serve as social proof. You can use them to confirm client claims and enhance promotional strategies. But how valuable is social proof for your brand?

Social Proof Builds Trust and Establishes Credibility

Social proof is vital for successful marketing and building customer trust. You can use customer feedback to boost sales and beat your competitors.

Online reviews are trusted by 80% of customers. This considerable percentage shows the feedback's effect on consumer choices. Also, customers read up to 10 reviews before purchasing. The same survey says positive feedback attracts 54% of website visitors (Shrestha et al., 2022).

Thus, as more and more customers trust online reviews, ensure you generate more positive feedback. This action plan will establish brand credibility.

Reviews Are the Focal Point of Social Proof

In 1984, Dr. Robert B. Cialdini introduced the concept of social proof. He highlighted the importance of people feeling confident when others make similar choices.

As an entrepreneur, ensure your business generates more positive reviews. But consumers see third-party platforms as more credible and trustworthy. They know business owners like you can't control them. Thus, ensure your brand has 5-star reviews on these review platforms.

High consumer confidence makes your brand trustworthy. But customers are more likely to buy from you if they read positive reviews on third-party platforms.

How Third-Party Review Platforms Help Your Business

Today's technology makes it possible for online reviews to be relevant to your business. Your customers may use third-party review platforms to share their stories about using your product or service. Then, when potential customers read them, they now have a basis to make sound decisions.

But third-party review platforms aren't for customer feedback only. They also play a crucial part in boosting credibility and trust. For instance, clients rely on them to assess your company. They check if you offer quality products and services. Also, they investigate your reputation before buying. Third-party review platforms show your positive reviews, ratings, and testimonials. They help you outsmart your competitors and earn the trust of potential customers.

Let's explore various ways third-party review platforms can help your business.

How Online Reviews Boost Your Expertise, Authority, and Trustworthiness

Google's Expertise, Authority, and Trustworthiness (EAT) impacts search rankings by prioritizing informative, reliable content.

To rank higher, you should meet the EAT criteria. You can do so by partnering with reputable review sites for positive external reviews. Over time, these reviews can enhance your brand's trustworthiness.

But not all third-party review sites are worth your time. You should only concentrate on those offering the best value.

Which Online Review Sites Are Most Significant?

You must gather customer feedback on many review platforms to enhance your success. Your Google reviews affect SEO and search results. Additionally, Facebook reaches a vast audience. Thus, collecting Facebook reviews can make people recognize your brand.

Yelp and Angi can help local businesses. Also, a BBB accreditation and high Trustpilot scores boost brand credibility. Industry-specific review sites may also be valuable. For instance, you can use the RealSelf review platform for the medical aesthetic industry.

Now you know which third-party review sites can help your business, you may ask how they can help your brand.

How Can You Use Online Reviews to Promote Your Brand?

Online reviews enhance brand management and trust. By using relevant keywords, customer feedback can boost your SEO ranking. Thus, focus on showcasing positive reviews and badges from review sites.

Now that you understand online reviews and how they can help your business, you should know why you must pursue feedback. So let's discuss the psychology of feedback next.

The Psychology of Reviews: Why Actively Pursuing Reviews Is Crucial

Customer frustration is a pressing concern and results in lower sales. Clients now discuss their disappointments with some brands, products, or services online. Thus, you should focus on online reviews to build connections and loyalty. To enhance customer experience, you must understand what your clients want.

You can analyze feedback from several sources to identify emotions during the customer journey. Check support tickets, social media, surveys, and reviews to help you.

Before we delve deeper, let's check the following statistics to help you understand the psychology of product reviews.

Vital Stats You Should Understand About the Psychology of Product Reviews

Ratings and reviews impact customer buying decisions. A 2021 Shopper Approved survey revealed most buyers prefer products from companies with 4.5 to 5-star ratings. They also choose items with more reviews among similarly rated products. Usually, buyers seek a minimum 4.5-star rating, while products with only 5-star reviews can seem suspicious (Sprague, 2021). Thus, you can find ways to achieve a high review rating without aiming for the perfect score. More customers will patronize your business because they now find you credible.

Types of Customer Reviews

We've been talking about customer reviews, but do you realize there are different types?

- *Company reviews* assess overall business quality, including delivery, customer experience, and order process. At the same time, *product reviews* focus on size, suitability, fit, and longevity.

- *Verified reviews*, confirmed by proof of purchase, are more reliable. Unfortunately, review platforms accept all feedback, including *unverified ones.*

Your customers write different types of reviews. But do you know how they can influence potential clients?

How Online Reviews Influence Your Customers

Product reviews are vital to understanding a brand's public perception. They're more trustworthy than marketing perspectives. Also, they promote transparency, trust, and social belonging, influencing sales and product improvement.

If you engage with reviews and address concerns, you can enhance customer loyalty and promote transparency. But how do you think these reviews can influence the customers? Feedback affects buying decisions. They offer personal experiences and connect readers to the brand.

But be careful about influencer or paid reviews because they may lack neutrality. It's best to allow your customers to write personalized reviews. They can help others understand product features and usage. As a result, they influence others' choices.

For example, you sell rice cookers worldwide. If most customer reviews say your products work only with 220V, American buyers will buy from other sellers because the US only supplies 120V.

For instance, you sell shirts, but most reviews suggest buying a size larger because your sizing is too small. Potential customers can buy a bigger size for a perfect fit when they read them. They can use the reviews as a basis for their buying decision.

How Reviews Affect the Customer's Buying Decision

Psychological factors affect customer choices. Reviews are akin to personal sentiments. Readers believe reviewers because they can relate with them. Thus, this reviewer–reader relationship can influence their perception. To maintain brand authenticity, you must analyze customer sentiment.

What You Can Learn From Sentiment Analysis

Sentiment analysis helps understand customer emotions and needs. It aids product improvement and addresses negative feedback. You can use review data to assess brand perception and enhance customer experience.

Also, sentiment analysis can inspire marketing ideas and new features while filling gaps in buyer journeys. But before you can analyze customer perception, people should first find your business. Using Google Map Pack can help.

The Importance of Google Map Pack

Google Maps helps users find businesses, boosting online and local presence. Focus on the Google Map Pack for its benefits and use it to generate leads for your company.

What Is a Google Map Pack?

Google Map Pack is crucial for search results of local businesses. It can help your business rank higher in local listings. To get started, you must provide essential info like address, hours, and contact details for business verification. Also, users can explore enterprises by calling or accessing directions through Google Maps.

How Google Map Pack Works

Google Map Pack displays top local business results based on its algorithm. Google Maps also ranks higher than traditional search results. Thus, using it and providing essential company information supports your SEO efforts.

The Significance of Google Map Pack for SEO

Google Map Pack expands the business reach and holds top local search positions. Using it boosts organic visits, calls, and competitiveness. It caters to mobile users and fosters enterprise growth.

Before you learn to use the Google Map Pack, you should know its attributes and qualities first.

Examining the Attributes and Qualities of Google Maps

Google Maps enhances user experience by simplifying interactions with local businesses. Critical elements in the Google Map Pack include business name, rating, price, address, hours, and more. But like your website, you need your Google Maps to rank for more people to see it.

Is There a Way to Boost Your Standing in Google Maps?

Guaranteeing a specific Google Map Pack position is impossible. Thus, you should improve your ranking by applying local SEO techniques. Focus on these five crucial factors, like a verified Google business listing:

Set Up Your Business Listing on Google

First, improve your Google local pack ranking by managing your Google Business Profile listing. Verify your company on the premier search engine by following these steps:

- Keep the business name simple.

- Fix errors and duplicates.

- Provide detailed information (hours, location, website, phone number).

- Write an engaging description.

- Maintain consistency in address format and local phone number.

- Upload high-quality photos weekly.

- Keep Google Business Profile information updated and accurate.

Enhance Your Listing to Gain Reviews

Second, responding to reviews enhances customer perceptions and proves business value. Thus, you should thoughtfully respond and address feedback to make your review oversight strategy successful.

Online reviews are vital for customers to discover reliable local businesses. They affect Google rankings, including the Google 3-Pack. Also, they establish trust and social proof and increase sales. But getting online reviews isn't enough. You should also get online citations.

Create Citations for Your Business

Third, you can create consistent citations on many platforms. This strategy boosts the online visibility of your business on Google Map Pack. Use a local listing management solution to handle many locations efficiently. Aside from citations, you can also attract more traffic through on-site SEO.

Tune Your Website to Increase Visibility in Google's Local Pack to Generate Greater Traffic

Fourth, improve your Google Map Pack position through on-site SEO by structuring and expanding your website for local SEO. Ensure your business name, address, and phone number (NAP) is available on all web pages.

You should also include unique local content like features, hours, news, promotions, team info, reviews, and local history. Add a Google map with the same address as your Google Business Profile listing on your

"Contact" or "About Us" page. Then, collaborate with your community to boost online visibility in Google Maps.

Connect With Your Community

Fifth, increase your Google Map Pack ranking by engaging with the local community. You can build strong neighborhood connections to establish local authority. By doing so, you also promote your online presence.

Another way of promoting online visibility is using the backlink strategy with noncompeting businesses. For instance, you can ask the local chamber of commerce to add your business to its website with a link to your site. Also, another technique of connecting with your community is to join local events and charities.

Now you know the importance of reviews and reputation management. Let me tell you an instance of how my consulting client dealt with negative reviews.

How I Helped My Consulting Client Deal With Negative Reviews

For a business owner, negative feedback is not unusual. Recently, a consulting client dealt with a customer complaint about experiencing pain in their eyelid after a procedure. I asked my client to speak to their customer to understand and resolve the issue immediately. After ensuring an amicable outcome, my client asked their customer to update their review to reflect the resolution.

You see, customer feedback can have a powerful impact on business success. Favorable reviews can attract more clients and increase revenue. At the same time, unfavorable ones can have the opposite effect. As an entrepreneur, you should deal with complaints to find acceptable solutions. This way, your business maintains an outstanding reputation.

Managing your reputation also involves responding to reviews and actively pursuing them. Knowing the psychology of feedback and reputation management can raise your income and get more reviews.

If you prefer to move forward, consider exploring *The Glowing Reviews Profit System.*

Chapter 2:

Overview of *The Glowing Reviews Profit System* Blueprint

Visualize this thing you want. See it, feel it, believe in it. Make your mental blueprint and begin. –Robert Collier

Do you still remember how you started your business? You were excited. You knew you could make it work. You were full of confidence because you were meticulous in crafting your business plan. Also, you understood the theoretical aspects of running a business. You greeted each morning with energy and enthusiasm.

But as you got into the daily grind of running your company, you realized it takes a lot of work. You dealt with problem after problem. You were exhausted. You've finished so many tasks, but your to-do list seems endless. Unfortunately, you didn't have much time. You started binge eating. Relationships turned sour because you didn't keep your promises.

You begin asking yourself, *When will all these issues end? When can I sit back and enjoy the gains of my business? Will I ever have time to relax?*

Everyone had to go through the same scenario as a new business owner. I know because I did. I faced the realities of business operations. I had to search for a means to cut expenses and boost revenue. My health suffered.

How did you feel when your customer gave your first customer review? Was it a positive one? I'm sure you were pleased because it validated the awesome things you're doing for your business. You were in high spirits for weeks. But do you remember the range of emotions you had when you got a negative review?

Reviews are vital to a thriving business. Positive ones reinforce your brand and can even encourage other customers to give more feedback. They also encourage others to patronize your company. They're your brand advocates who passed the word around about how you provide quality products or services.

But negative reviews are also essential because they improve the product or service quality. If you get a few, you shouldn't brush them off because they may discourage new customers from buying from you. Clients will see you as uncaring. Eventually, they will look for other vendors and stop doing business with you.

Customer feedback, in general, generates social proof. It helps others learn about your business. Also, it improves SEO rankings because more and more customers mention your brand online. Thus, you should encourage buyers to write reviews about your product, service, or company.

Reviews improve your brand trustworthiness. If you leverage resources like the Google Map Pack, you also increase the online visibility of your business. Because customer reviews matter, you should strive to pursue them.

As an entrepreneur, you must actively pursue customers to give reviews. Also, focus on managing your reputation daily. You may have noticed that unsatisfied customers have the motivation to write complaints about your business. But satisfied clients rarely write praises.

Thus, you should work hard on pursuing satisfied clients to give positive reviews to counter the bad ones you get. You don't want negative feedback to outnumber positive ones, so make it a point to pursue reviews actively.

Of course, you can only generate positive feedback if you satisfy your customers. Focus on delivering high-quality goods or services if you want your clients to write quality reviews.

Aside from providing quality products and services, you should ensure your employees are professional and happy. If you're a good employer, your staff will strive to reciprocate your goodness by being good to your customers. They'll be good communicators when clients complain or ask questions.

The Glowing Reviews Profit System consists of 10 core steps you should follow every day if you want your business to thrive:

1. Aim to deliver a 5-star experience every day. Know the customers' needs and demands. Then, strive hard to exceed their expectations. Treat your employees as your treasure. This way, they'll work hard to satisfy your client's requirements. Give your staff the benefits they deserve to make them happy.

2. Tell your employees to interview new customers to ask how they knew about your business. Always engage your clients through email or text, but ensure they give you express approval. Craft a short survey, and be ready with a follow-up question.

   Once you know how your customers learned about your business, you can use that information to focus your marketing initiatives on the most appropriate channels they use to find you. This way, you save your resources for channels that will deliver a return.

3. Use social media to engage your customers. Be where your clients are. This way, it's easier for them to give reviews. Simplify the process by sharing links. Also, train your employees to become brand advocates by empowering them. For example, your front desk staff can ask customers about their experience with your business.

4. Assess customer satisfaction through available metrics. You must forge an emotional bond with your clients to ensure they have a fantastic experience patronizing your business. Set realistic targets for customer satisfaction scores.

5. Make it a habit to always ask for reviews. You can use various techniques to generate customer feedback. Aside from your website, you can also seek requests on third-party customer feedback platforms. This way, potential clients encounter you, and they'll most likely search for feedback about a brand, product, or service.

6. Always respond to reviews on your website, social media, and other platforms. But ensure you do it immediately and use keywords for SEO purposes. If your business gets 1-, 2-, or 3-star reviews, you must contact the reviewers to understand their issues. Try to resolve their problems, and ask them to update their review if you've successfully resolved them.

7. If you want more reviews, you should remove the barriers for customers who try to write feedback. Make it easier for them by providing links and sharing their feedback. But ensure you read the "Terms of Service" of third-party review platforms before initiating the incentives.

8. Always remember to share positive customer reviews on social media. Doing so will establish trust in your brand. Also, if clients are unsure of patronizing you, they will have confidence in buying from you because of the positive reviews you share. Your new clients will also know what to expect from your product or service through the positive feedback of satisfied customers.

9. You can use customer feedback to improve your business. Ask your clients what features they want in your product. They'll appreciate you because they know you value what they have to say. Do your best to provide the ultimate customer experience to encourage repeat purchases.

10. Use tech tools for efficient collection and response to customer reviews. These apps and platforms can effortlessly integrate with your other business tools. You can scout for a customer review management application to help you with client feedback.

The Glowing Reviews Profit System is an approach you can use to boost your profits. It focuses on generating positive customer feedback to understand and resolve client issues. Clients often feel valued if you approach them. You may even transform negative reviews into positive ones if you strive to solve their problems.

This methodology is encompassing. It deals with customers and employees. Keep your staff happy by empowering them and providing the necessary benefits and training.

Also, *The Glowing Reviews Profit System* deals with you as an entrepreneur. Concentrate on your overall well-being to run your business efficiently. Practice the 10 core steps daily to see your company grow and generate higher profits.

We'll talk about the details of each step in the succeeding sections. Let's start with the first step!

Chapter 3:

Step 1—Craft a 5-Star Customer Experience

Customers who love you will market for you more powerfully than you can possibly market yourself. –Jeanne Bliss

Exceptional customer service is crucial for setting your business apart from your competitors. According to Harvard Business Review, organizations with consistently high customer satisfaction ratings for three or more years have significantly faster revenue growth than their competitors (Markey, n.d.). Thus, if you want your business to thrive, you should consistently get high customer satisfaction scores. You must enhance the customer experience by delivering top-notch service. Also, you must meet or exceed client expectations.

Here's how you can provide top-notch service to your clients.

Meeting and Exceeding Client Expectations

Ensure to exceed customer expectations and provide prompt, personalized service. If you do so, your clients will keep patronizing your brand.

A Salesforce survey revealed that 71% of respondents would find other suppliers if they were unhappy with a company (Afshar, 2022). Thus, understand and exceed customer expectations to keep your customers.

Types of Customer Expectations

Identify your client's expectations and needs to develop compelling customer engagement strategies. But first, know the various kinds of customer expectations:

- *Implicit expectations* are about past experiences with competitors.

- *Static performance expectations* focus on a company's reliability, accessibility, and customization.

- *Explicit expectations* refer to customers' preferences for a product or service.

- *Interpersonal expectations* relate to the customer's expectation about the staff's tone of communication.

- *Dynamic performance expectations* anticipate how a product or service will change and evolve.

To succeed in any business, you must offer a positive customer experience. Some companies try to meet their client's expectations as they deliver their goods and services. But those aspiring to be the best know that meeting client expectations alone is insufficient.

Consequently, surpassing those expectations is possible if you offer superior-quality solutions. But why should you aim for it?

Top Reasons for Customer Service to Exceed Client Expectations

You may wonder why your customer service should exceed customer expectations. Here are three reasons:

Competitive Advantages

Quality customer support is vital for business competitiveness. It sets your company apart from your rivals. Thus, focus on providing exceptional user experiences for new clients. How? You can hire skilled, friendly support staff and train them thoroughly to provide the best experiences to your clients. If you do, satisfied customers will remember and recommend your services.

Creates Loyalty

Focus on providing top-quality support services to build customer loyalty. You should consistently deliver exceptional experiences to earn your customers' trust.

You should have a system for providing customer support. Once it's in place, have your staff follow it. Your customers will be raving about the top-notch service they receive from you. To encourage repeat business, strive to meet or exceed customers' expectations.

Word-of-Mouth Advertising

Satisfied customers will share their experiences to influence potential clients. Thus, word-of-mouth advertising is a powerful, cost-effective marketing tool. If you provide exceptional customer service, you generate positive feedback. This type of advertising is more powerful than the traditional ones.

Advertising, marketing, and past experiences shape customer expectations. Thus, you must identify customer touchpoints and provide the best experiences to meet customer demands.

But how do you identify these customer demands?

How to Identify Your Customers' Needs and Demands

To offer outstanding customer service, understanding the customers' expectations is crucial. Communication plays a significant role in realizing their needs and wants. Follow these tips to uncover their expectations:

Ask Your Customers

You can ask your clients through email surveys or individual interviews. Include questions like rating their experience, recommendations, and suggestions for improvement. This approach shows you value their needs.

Ask Your Team of Customer Service Representatives

Aside from asking your customers, you can gather insights from your employees. Do so through virtual meetings, in-person team meetings, one-on-one sessions, or surveys. Remember to encourage employee input to enhance customer experiences further.

Do Your Research

Another way is to research competitors' online activities and customer feedback. You can compare business models to identify improvement areas.

Analyze reviews on various platforms, but be aware of potential biases. If you understand and meet customer expectations, you ensure the success of your business.

Once you know your customer's expectations, you can plan on exceeding them.

How to Exceed Customer Expectations

As an entrepreneur, it is critical to concentrate on customer satisfaction. Consider implementing the following tips to ensure a constant inflow of positive feedback.

Listen to Your Customer

First, be familiar with your customers. By showing interest in their hobbies and family, you can understand their goals and how your business can help them. This connection boosts their confidence in your services.

Expect and Meet the Customer Needs

Second, offer valuable guidance to customers needing clarification about what they want. Check the following steps to anticipate your client's goals:

- Conduct thorough marketing research.
- Stay up-to-date with trends.
- Familiarize yourself with psychological principles.
- Get to know your client better.
- Maintain open communication about any concerns.

Be Sincere and Honest With Your Customer

Third, you should be transparent about business limitations. Honesty in managing client expectations is vital. Also, focus on improving the product or service rather than making false promises. Truthful delivery of what's possible is critical.

Fulfill Your Promises

Fourth, as a business owner, be realistic about your strengths and avoid making unachievable promises. To prevent client disappointments, ensure the feasibility of your commitments.

Provide Ways for Your Customer to Solve Their Issues

Fifth, offer troubleshooting guides and self-serve phone menus. Customers seek convenient solutions. Thus, you should provide popular self-help options. But ensure these alternatives are user-friendly to maintain customer satisfaction.

Here are some methods to achieve this:

Create a Chatbot

You can provide chatbots that can interact with customers with programmed responses. They provide specific solutions or subtopics based on the chosen inquiry topic.

Prepare a Knowledge Database

Another method is to make information and solutions available to your customers. You can create a knowledge database they can access at their convenience.

Create a Community Forum

Lastly, offer a digital platform for customer interaction through a community forum. Forum visitors can join the product discussions and strengthen the online community.

To provide a top-quality customer experience, strive to exceed client expectations. It is also crucial to focus on the professionalism and happiness of your employees. The following section will discuss how to achieve this.

The Power of Happy, Professional Staff

Pursuing happiness is vital to everyone, and people in different industries are more aware of it now than ever. All age groups see this trend, and people are willing to change jobs to find happiness in their personal lives and at work. Thus, you should strive to make your employees happy.

What Benefits Do You Gain if You Have Happy Employees?

Keeping your staff comfortable is the correct thing to do. Your team doesn't only gain from it. You also do. Here are some vital advantages of having a motivated staff:

Increased Productivity

First, focus on making your employees happy because it boosts productivity. Research reported that staff satisfaction could increase productivity by 12%. At the same time, employee distress can decrease productivity by 10% (Oswald, 2015).

Contented staff concentrate more on their work and take fewer breaks. Unfortunately, unhappy and stressed employees are more distracted and less engaged.

High Employee Engagement

Second, employee engagement is also vital to business success. Engaged employees are enthusiastic and eager to make valuable contributions. Also, employee satisfaction is critical in fostering engagement. A happy employee is more likely to meet the company's goals.

Improved Creativity

Third, happy employees are more committed to their work and better understand the organization's goals. As such, they produce innovative ideas and suggestions that could benefit the business. Also, you can pursue innovation if your employees feel secure to take risks to unleash their creativity.

Low Absenteeism

Fourth, unhappy employees need to have more dedication toward work. They are likely to skip work leading to increased absenteeism. But content employees are passionate about their jobs and motivated to arrive on time.

Improved Retention

Fifth, happy employees don't leave their jobs. The Development Academy's study found that over 75% of dissatisfied workers search for other jobs. But content employees are less likely to look elsewhere for work (Richardson, 2022). If you want to cut costs in training new staff, strive to make your employees happy.

Now you understand why you should maintain a happy workforce, but have you ever wondered what makes your employees unhappy?

Why Is Your Staff Unhappy (and How You Can Turn It Around)?

A survey by Mental Health America revealed four main reasons for workplace dissatisfaction (Hellebuyck et al., 2017):

- lack of job security

- insufficient pay

- lack of acknowledgment

- poor assistance from coworkers and superiors

Let's discuss each one.

Job Insecurity

Job security positively affects employee satisfaction, while insecurity negatively affects it. As an employer, you can foster open communication and empower your staff with special projects. Also, you must offer fair pay and benefits to improve job satisfaction.

Low Salary

Employee compensation impacts satisfaction and performance, being a significant expense for companies. Consider the following factors when addressing salary issues:

- tenure

- job role

- education

- training

Also, you should show your commitment to employee happiness and retention.

Lack of Recognition

In *How to Be Happy at Work*, Annie Mckee explains that employee happiness and engagement decrease when feeling ignored (Knight, 2017). At the same time, recognition boosts productivity and promotes a better work culture.

You can encourage appreciation by acknowledging employees' daily efforts. Also, you should highlight their contributions in presentations and reports.

Lack of Support

A robust workplace support system significantly affects employee productivity. Avoid negative feedback and condescending behavior. Instead, promote mentorship, open communication, and growth opportunities. This alternative creates a positive environment, reduces stress, and boosts happiness and productivity.

Crafting a 5-star customer experience has a three-pronged approach. We've already discussed meeting and exceeding customer expectations and keeping your employees happy. The last method is about consistency in the delivery of superior service.

Delivering Superior Service Consistently

Ever considered your top customer service encounter? Maybe a barista recalled your name and latte preference, or a support agent exceeded expectations in resolving your issue. Good experiences foster positive company perception and customer loyalty. Thus, as an entrepreneur, you must provide consistent, superior service to keep these loyal customers.

Qualities of Superior Customer Service

Offering outstanding customer service is crucial in today's aggressive market. It involves addressing clients' queries and problems and building an emotional connection. Also, it includes understanding and surpassing their expectations and demonstrating empathy.

This section explores the qualities of superior customer service and how to use them in your business. So let's discover the secrets to providing outstanding customer service.

Responsiveness

First, acknowledge service requests and respond to customers immediately. The Customer Service Benchmark report said 62% of businesses don't reply to customer emails (MacDonald, 2023).

To consistently deliver top-notch service, ensure you respond to them immediately. Also, ensure you establish your presence in various support channels.

Speed and Efficiency

Second, customers expect prompt and efficient service. A CMO Council study found good customer service involves quick response. It also includes resolving issues on the first contact (Choksi, 2017). Thus, you should provide efficient and prompt service. Solve the case the first time the client reported it. Customers hate contacting a company for the same problem repeatedly.

Competence

Third, frontline employees must have the professional competence to deliver top-notch customer service. ThinkJar reports 84% of customers feel annoyed when service agents lack skill. Also, nearly one third of them switch brands due to poor staff knowledge (Afshar, 2015).

Courtesy

Fourth, common courtesy is essential for delivering top-notch customer service. When dealing with customers, your staff must be polite and friendly. Ensure they follow proper service etiquette.

Remember that the level of courtesy exhibited by employees affects the customer's experience. A survey reported 73% of consumers would be loyal to a brand if employees were friendly (RightNow Technologies, 2012).

Consistency

Lastly, consistent provision of positive customer experiences across various channels is vital. As per McKinsey & Company, seamless, unified service at all touchpoints boost customer satisfaction and trust (Deshpande, n.d.).

How I Improve the Customer Experience in My Consulting Clients' Businesses

One way of improving customer service is to ask your staff to try your competitors' products and services. You can also try them if you have time. This way, you will know which policies to include in your business. Also, this strategy helps your staff to realize the significance of providing a superior customer experience.

For example, you can give Spafinder gift cards as a reward to your employees. They can enjoy your competitor's services and report their experience to you. This way, you can enhance your services too. My consulting clients also find this technique helpful. Why don't you try it and see if it works?

Your business can gain from providing superior customer service. To achieve this, you must meet and exceed customer expectations consistently. Also, you should create a positive work environment and have a dedicated staff delivering superior service.

You can increase your loyal customers and get ahead of your competitors. Also, quality customer service generates positive online reviews and referrals. It can help in increasing revenue and boosting business growth.

But before building a loyal customer base, you should find out how your customers find your business. Why? You'll learn about it next.

Chapter 4:

Step 2—Inquire How a Client Found You

The customer's perception is your reality. –Kate Zabriskie

Tracking the source of paying customers can be crucial for the growth of your business. Thus, you must identify which marketing channels or advertising sources are efficient. Then, focus on improving or eliminating the ones that aren't.

A simple technique to track this is to ask clients how they learned about your company. While conversing with each customer is ideal, it may sometimes be impossible.

This step will discuss the whys and hows of asking how your clients found you. Let's dive into the reasons first.

Why You Should Ask How Clients Found You

It's essential to know how your clients discovered you. Otherwise, you might miss an opportunity to enhance your most effective marketing channel. At the same time, you also waste resources on ineffective methods. Also, you can assess the effectiveness of your marketing campaign if you know how your customers found you.

As a business, you put in extra effort to advertise your brand, but how do you determine which tactics are effective when customers approach you? Could it be your email campaigns or social media marketing? Is it from your word-of-mouth referrals or favorable search engine results?

The most straightforward approach to finding out is by asking your customers. It is precisely what the "How Did You Hear About Us" survey aims to do. Explain to your customers that their response will help you improve your business and offer a better experience.

But how do you create a survey? You'll learn how next!

How to Craft a Survey About "How Did You Find Us?"

When you include the question "How did you learn about us?" in your survey or form, there are different approaches you can use. To ensure respondents can express their opinions fully, offer all possible options to allow them to choose their answers.

But this approach often results in incomplete or nonsensical answers. People don't see much value in this question and want to move on. To avoid getting many "Don't remember" or "NA" answers, you can include those places where you advertised. It is simple for respondents as they have to click one of the options.

But what options can you provide, and how do you account for those who don't remember? Here are some typical alternatives you can use:

Select a Distribution Channel for Your Survey

Your first option is to choose where you'll distribute your survey. It's essential to consider the channels that have successfully reached out to your customers. You can stick with the alternatives that have already worked for you, such as website pop-ups, in-app surveys, text messages, and emails. Developing something new is unnecessary if you're already seeing results.

Decide on a Survey Template

Next, pick a template. Professionals specializing in customer feedback created the survey template for "How did you hear about us?" It aims to receive a high response rate and uses survey logic to show follow-up questions based on the respondent's answers. You can customize it by changing the wording, translating it, or adding or deleting questions to fit your needs.

Consider a Follow-Up Question

After deciding on the template, prepare follow-up questions. Users prefer simple answers over complex ones due to the economy of effort. They are unlikely to exert much effort on an action that doesn't benefit them. If you've asked a question on your website, you may have noticed people often give minimalistic answers.

While this may be acceptable sometimes, it won't give you more profound insights. Thus, it's crucial to have follow-up questions for clients to explain their answers. This practice holds when asking how they found out about your business.

Multiple-choice boxes are an excellent way to approach this issue. You can get informative answers without wasting customers' time. Since you only provide limited options, this technique is suitable for follow-up survey questions.

Examples of Follow-Up Survey Questions

If you want to collect details about how your customers first interacted with your business, I have some questions you can ask:

"Which Google Search Did You Use to Find Us?"

Using this as a follow-up for those who mentioned finding you through a search engine is advisable. This inquiry can also assist with keyword research and SEO, particularly if you need to use more costly SEO tools. Also, knowing the search terms leading them to you can help you enhance your content for better rankings on Google Search.

"Did You Find Your Answers From Us?"

I have a straightforward yet efficient inquiry on my frequently visited web pages. I use it to gauge the quality of the content and identify opportunities to offer our visitors added value.

If the response is negative, I ask another question, "What else can we assist you with?" This question comes with predefined options and an open field where visitors can provide their answers.

This tactic has generated more leads from my blog as we offer visitors extra content as a lead magnet, which they requested.

"Would You Consider Engaging With Us or Referring Us to Your Friends?"

This question will help you assess their satisfaction level with their initial experience. It will assist you in computing your Net Promoter Score (NPS). Please note you can only ask it after some time because you may overwhelm your customers.

Determine the Context

After preparing the follow-up questions, focus on determining the context. To enhance the effectiveness of your inquiry, know the circumstances under which your clients found you. For example, you solve various customer issues as a provider of services or products. Besides learning how they found you, you can also inquire about what they sought when they arrived on your website.

It will help you determine whether they were looking for a solution to a problem or popular businesses in your industry. They may also search for a new skill or a replacement for their current product or service.

Understanding the context of your "How did you hear about us?" question will enable you to create content catering to their needs. Additionally, if they discovered you through a website or platform, you can give more time and resources to these channels.

Create a Budget

Once you understand where your customers found your company, update your budget accordingly. Efficient marketing dictates you discard ineffective channels.

Analyze the information to decide which channels need more funding and which you should discard. As a result, it will offer a leaner marketing mix and a higher gain from your marketing investment.

Use Third-Party Tools

After you have created the survey, it is crucial to integrate it with any useful third-party tools. Survicate offers a variety of built-in integrations, like Slack, HubSpot, Intercom, and Smartlook. These integrations allow instant notifications if there are new survey responses. They also automate various processes.

Continue Monitoring and Analyzing

The practice of asking new customers how they found you should be an ongoing project because you should continuously improve. Make data-based changes and perform further analysis to boost your campaign. From your research, you can then identify exciting growth opportunities.

Other Ways to Find Out How Your Customers Discovered You

You could simplify your marketing strategies if you know how customers found your business. You can also attract more potential clients with the information you gathered. Also, asking how they found you uncover new avenues for reaching customers.

Several other methods are available to understand how customers learn about your company. Let's discuss some of them.

Ask Your Customers

It is typical for satisfied customers to share how they discovered your business. You can get this information by training your employees to ask during face-to-face interactions. Also, you can allow customers to share their source of discovery when making purchases or registering for events online.

Use Search Engines

Look for your company name on popular search engines. It will show you where your business information is available online. Expect to find your business on online listing platforms, review sites, and social networks.

After searching for your company, try using search terms that could drive more people to your business. For instance, if you own a restaurant business, you could try using the following search terms:

- "Restaurants in [your town]"

- "[Type of cuisine] in [your town]"

- "Places to eat in [your town]"

Or if you own a mechanic shop, you could try using search terms such as the following:

- "Where to get my car fixed in [your town]"

- "Mechanics in [your town]"

- "Car shop in [your town]"

- "Where to get [particular repair or service] in [your town]"

Once you generate a list of all the places where your business is already showing up, note down any areas where your business should be. This way, you can publish your business information on those sites.

Use Google Analytics

Google Analytics lets you understand your website's traffic. You gain a robust understanding of your audience's interaction with your blog or site. With Google Analytics, you can determine the following:

- pages that generate the most traffic

- where that traffic comes from

- which devices your audience uses to access your site.

Additionally, Google Analytics lets you see how long people spend on each page. It gives you valuable information on how people find you and what resources they use to research your business.

Observe Your Audience

Only some people who check out your Facebook Page or Twitter account will necessarily become your fan or follower. But you should still keep track of changes in your audience. It can give you valuable insight into which platforms are most suitable for your business.

Focus on your customers' reactions to your activity. For example, if a post generates a lot of shares and attracts new fans, consider incorporating similar content into your future posts. Additionally, pay attention to how your interactions with people affect your fan and follower counts.

Track Your Email List

Using sign-up tools to expand your email list lets you conveniently keep tabs on where individuals sign up within your account. Moreover, it lets you track your email list's growth online and how people join it offline.

These individuals aren't just discovering your business and taking action to stay connected. So it's crucial to simplify the sign-up process to hasten the growth of your email list. Do so to bring you closer to attracting your next ideal customer.

Sample Survey: How Did You Find Us?

The placement and wording of your survey question will depend on the context triggering it. You should be mindful of the timing and ensure the question flows seamlessly with the other questions.

How did you discover us?

- Search engine

- Publication or blog

- Social media

- Recommended by a colleague, friend, or family member

- Other, please specify: _____

This survey is a basic illustration of a "How did you find us?" questionnaire. It inquires about the source from which the participant found the company and offers five options.

It helps collect data before (such as when checking out) or after (such as in the order confirmation email) purchasing.

The question "How did you know about us?" is practical only for those businesses making the extra effort to enhance the user's experience. Following the steps will increase your survey completion rates and the quality of responses you receive.

You do not need marketing or data analysis skills to create this survey question. All you need is a survey question, and you can get information about your customers' sources of information in as little as 5 minutes.

Now you know where your customers first heard about your business, your next goal is to assess customer satisfaction. The next step will help you.

Chapter 5:

Step 3—Assess Customer Satisfaction

The basics of business is to stay as close as possible to your customers—understand their behavior, their preferences, their purchasing patterns, etc. –Indra Nooyi

It's essential to check how happy your customers are to make your business better and more profitable. This step teaches you about measuring customer satisfaction and using that info to improve your company.

Surveys are an excellent strategy to know what's inside your customers' heads and make tweaks to help your business grow. You'll also learn how satisfied customers are more likely to become loyal clients and get tips on keeping them coming back for more.

How to Assess Customer Satisfaction

When running a business, trusting your gut feeling alone to keep your customers happy won't cut it anymore.

Regularly checking in with your clients is crucial to ensure customer satisfaction.

Measuring client happiness can help you save time and money on support resources. So let's chat about why keeping tabs on your customers' feelings is essential!

Why Measure Customer Satisfaction

Want to know a secret to increasing brand loyalty and reducing price sensitivity? Form a solid emotional bond with your customers! Focus on their needs and provide a positive experience to boost competitiveness and retention. They'll reward you by becoming frequent buyers if they realize you prioritize them.

Although cost is a factor, most consumers focus on their encounter with a product, service, or brand. During tough financial times, customers may seek alternatives. Their finances may no longer support buying their current brands.

But word-of-mouth recommendations can significantly impact consumer sales. Satisfied customers can advocate for your products and services. Thus, you must concentrate on providing the utmost customer satisfaction. Also, ensure you constantly assess customer needs to make your clients happy.

So let's get started on learning about measuring customer satisfaction effectively!

How to Gauge Customer Satisfaction

Let's dive into the six crucial metrics that can help your business succeed by keeping your customers happy. These metrics include the following:

- emotional and rational reactions to your brand

- behavioral intentions

- satisfaction scores that your customers determined themselves

You can ensure customer satisfaction and business growth by keeping track of these six metrics:

Customer Satisfaction Score

One of these metrics is the customer satisfaction score (CSAT). You can create surveys after customers buy from you to assess their happiness about their experience. These surveys can use numbers or fun emojis to rate their encounter, and the scores range from 0–100%. If you're lucky, you can even ask follow-up questions to help improve things.

Net Promoter Score

The second metric is the Net Promoter Score (NPS). It's a nifty tool that helps businesses measure customer loyalty by asking how likely they are to recommend a brand. Based on reviewers' responses, it categorizes customers as promoters, passives, or detractors.

With NPS, you can gauge overall loyalty or specific experiences by tweaking the question using a 0–10 scale. You can also add open-ended queries in your NPS surveys to gain valuable insights on improving your business.

Customer Effort Score

For the third metric, customer effort score (CES) is a quick and easy way to measure how much effort your customers put in when engaging with your company. It shows how easy or hard it is for them to meet their objectives with your brand.

To improve your customer service, you can send out CES surveys after each interaction to get feedback and see where you can make things smoother. Plus, sharing this feedback with your team can help them provide even better support in the future!

Customer Churn Rate

The fourth metric is the customer churn rate you should use to measure customer satisfaction. It's always tough when clients are unhappy with your brand. No worries! You can always figure out why they're leaving. By analyzing the number of customers who drop out, you can get a feel for overall satisfaction levels and work to reduce churn. Here's how you can calculate your churn rate:

- Choose a time frame to analyze.

- Take the final customer count and subtract it from the initial count.

- Divide the resulting digit by the starting number of customers.

Customer Health Score

For the fifth metric, customer health score (CHS) is a handy tool that helps businesses measure customer loyalty by looking at a few key factors:

- How often do they buy from you?

- How much is their budget?

- How often do they contact your customer support team?

The great thing about CHS is that you can tailor it to each business. But the goal is always the same: to group customers into weak, at-risk, and robust categories. It's easy to focus on specific groups and give them the attention they need.

Customer Lifetime Value

The sixth metric is the customer lifetime value (CLTV). It's the total revenue you earn from one client from when they start buying from you to when they shift to another brand. But don't worry, calculating it is super easy! You must follow these simple steps:

1. Find the yearly average purchase value by dividing the actual dollars spent by the number of transactions.

2. Determine the annual purchase frequency by dividing the total transactions by the number of customers who bought from you. Combine these two figures to get the yearly average customer value.

3. Find the average customer life span.

4. Multiply the life span by the annual average customer value.

Now, let's talk about customer satisfaction. You can quickly assess it with specific objectives and set targets. Adjust accordingly based on your analysis. If you find your efforts are not enhancing your satisfaction rating, don't worry. Consider where to improve and set your targets as key performance indicators (KPIs).

How to Set Realistic Targets for Customer Satisfaction Ratings

In today's cutthroat market, keeping satisfied customers is crucial for any business to be successful. But do you know how to assess client satisfaction accurately? The secret is to set targets forcing you to improve while being practical. So let's delve into customer satisfaction ratings and discover the three secrets to setting targets.

Boost Your Customer Satisfaction Score

Ensure your customers are always happy by constantly improving their experience with you. It's essential to regularly check how you're doing in key areas and understand why your scores are the way they are. And remember to get input from other people involved in the process. Keep up with changing expectations and make your customers happy, even if you're already doing well!

Consider Your Competition

Want to ensure your customers are delighted when transacting with you? One effective technique is to check your competitors. By focusing on businesses prioritizing customer satisfaction, you can set goals for your company to meet or exceed.

Use Industry Benchmarks

Customer satisfaction has reliable benchmarks to gauge how satisfied your customers are. And to make them even happier, you can implement some practical strategies. Doing so will meet their expectations and boost your business growth.

Strategies for Increasing Business Performance Using Customer Satisfaction

Let's discuss the best techniques for obtaining client satisfaction details. And once you have this valuable information, how can you use it to improve your customers' happiness? We'll explore practical ways to assess customer satisfaction and boost their overall experience.

Use Agile Surveys in Measuring Customer Satisfaction

Collecting customer satisfaction data and setting KPIs are very important. But analyzing the data can be time-consuming. That's why using an agile approach to improve consumer sentiment monitoring is a good idea.

You can use efficient survey methods to get targeted and actionable insights. It's not enough to do assessments periodically. Continuous reviews are much better! They help you assess how customers respond to new products or system integrations.

Additionally, they can help you spot changes in customer sentiment. This feedback mechanism allows you to identify customer satisfaction trends. Plus, it will enable you to highlight your brand's best features.

Listen to Your Customers

While customer satisfaction ratings are helpful, they only give part of the picture. That's where natural language understanding (NLU) and conversational analytics are handy!

By using these tools, you can grasp your customers' emotions. Positive emotions increase ratings and repeat business. At the same time, negative experiences can hurt your overall satisfaction. So ensure you're using customer feedback to enhance your business!

Take Steps to Improve Customer Satisfaction

One way to boost client satisfaction is to determine what's causing their discontent. You can use real-time analytics solutions to address it. It's vital to constantly improve your processes based on customer preferences.

Surveys are another great way to boost customer engagement, especially in competitive markets. But how do you gather and understand what your customers think?

Steps to Understanding Customer Sentiment

When it comes to your internal procedures, it's essential to make sure you know your customers' emotions. Here are the top five stages you should follow to ensure you're implementing the necessary actions.

Collect Information

It's essential to keep track of their feedback using surveys, social media, and direct communication. And now, with conversational analytics, you can even assess their emotions and sentiments in real time! By combining all this data, you'll accurately measure customer satisfaction.

Understand the Effects of Customer Journey Touchpoints

One way to know the customer journey starts with satisfaction surveys. Know the touchpoints to make informed decisions and resolve problems.

Limit the Customer Satisfaction Drivers

To grow your business, know what your clients think. For example, you know that excellent communication is critical. Thus, ensure you're responding quickly, solving problems fast, and keeping everyone in the loop. And don't forget nobody likes waiting around or hearing the same thing repeatedly!

Empower Your Staff to Act

Improve client satisfaction by adapting internal procedures and empowering your employees. Create a proactive environment prioritizing customer happiness. To achieve this, use tools to keep track of any recurring customer concerns and share insights with the team.

Automate Your Activities

Technology can simplify processes and make them more efficient. It's also important to promptly address customer dissatisfaction. Also, communicate relevant information to the right groups.

You can handle more significant, strategic concerns by focusing on the small details. Automation and tools can make a difference in measuring customer satisfaction.

Reasons for Using Automation Tools for Customer Satisfaction Measurement

By automating how your team shares information, you can prevent errors and tackle dissatisfaction. But how will you recognize if your clients are upbeat with your brand? You can track social media, conduct focus groups, and analyze retention data.

Steps to Measure Customer Satisfaction

Don't worry about feeling overwhelmed when evaluating client happiness! Making customer satisfaction assessments a part of your success strategy simplifies your life. Follow these seven steps to ensure you gauge client satisfaction properly.

Create a Plan

First, devise a plan for measuring client satisfaction. If you want your team to succeed, creating a strategy focusing on these five key initiatives is crucial:

- Improve the user experience.

- Provide faster support for unhappy customers.

- Offer helpful information through knowledge bases and education.

- Try out new live chat and support methods.

- Use NPS to turn happy customers into big fans.

Decide on a Customer Satisfaction Survey

Second, pick a customer satisfaction survey. If you want to find out how happy your customers are, the first step is to talk to the people who make the big decisions in your company. Once you've got their input, it's time to decide on the questions you'll ask in your survey.

Tailor-Fit the Survey's Questions and Layout to Your Needs

Third, personalize the survey questions to fit your needs. Shorter surveys get better completion rates, so keep it concise and skip any unnecessary questions. And of course, always remember to respect your customers' time!

If you need to ask more in-depth questions, offer an incentive to encourage more participation and data collection. You'll earn some kudos for your efforts.

Establish Your Survey's Trigger

Fourth, learn how to set the trigger. You should ensure your surveys hit the sweet spot to get the most value and usefulness from your collected data. To do that, ensure you target the correct customers at the right time.

Otherwise, you risk getting low response rates and missing essential insights. Try to follow this schedule when sending NPS surveys:

- seven days after sign up

- thirty days after the first survey

- every ninety days during the customer life cycle

Select a Survey Method

Fifth, you should decide how to distribute your survey. When collecting client feedback, you can use the following popular methods:

- extended email surveys

- on-site or in-app surveys

- post-purchase or post-service surveys

You may need a specific tool or software to implement any survey methodologies.

Perform Data Analysis

Sixth, analyze the information you gathered. With NPS tools, you can easily categorize and integrate it with other products. You can take tailored actions for each segment of your audience.

Adjust and Repeat

Seventh, use valuable insights to identify the causes of dissatisfaction, and implement improvements. Also, remember to team up with your loyal supporters and work together on advocacy initiatives. By doing so, you can accurately gauge customer satisfaction and create an environment for high scores.

Sample Survey: Customer Satisfaction

Choose your survey questions from the examples below:

Product Usage

- How long have you used the product?

- How frequently do you use our brand?

- Which tool or aspect do you like the most?

- What features are most valuable to you?

- Are there any hardships faced while patronizing the product?

Demographics

- What is your age and location?

- What is your employment status?

- What is your highest education level?

- What is your company and job title?

Psychographics

- Do you prefer shopping via phone or laptop?

- What hardships do you face [product-related aspect]?

- What features do you dislike about [product type]?

- Please share your thoughts on [product type].

Satisfaction Scale

- Rate your satisfaction with today's store visit (on a scale of 1–10).

- Would you recommend us?

- Will you revisit our website?

Free-Form Text

- Share your thoughts on [company name or product].

- Describe us in one word, and feel free to add any comments.

Longevity

Are you open to chatting with a customer success manager? How about receiving product upgrade info and accessing resources for optimal usage?

To help your business grow, consider your customers' feelings about your brand. Asking for feedback through surveys can lead to positive changes within your company. By assessing customer satisfaction, you can build stronger customer loyalty and even see an increase in profits.

You now know how to assess customer satisfaction. Your next step is to discover where your customers are to engage them. How? Head to the next section to find out.

Chapter 6:

Step 4—Engage Where Clients Are and Rake in Reviews

A satisfied customer is the best business strategy of all. –Michael LeBoeuf

As an entrepreneur, actively engage with clients and simplify the review process to boost revenue. Use platforms like Facebook and Google and staff advocacy to encourage client feedback.

You can improve your stature and engage new customers through consistent positive reviews. Also, you should choose the right platform for customer feedback.

Finding the Right Platforms: Facebook, Google, and Beyond

Facebook, Google, YouTube, and Yelp are popular platforms for generating customer reviews. Know how to take advantage of each to boost client feedback. Let's start with Facebook first.

What You Should Know About Facebook Reviews

Facebook Recommendations benefit local businesses by enhancing their online presence and search visibility. Ultimately, they attract more customers.

Key research findings include the following:

- Facebook holds 19% of customer feedback, ranking fourth after Google, Yelp, and Tripadvisor (Bassig, 2022).

- Last year, 18.3% of U.S. adults purchased from Facebook Marketplace (Enberg, 2021).

- Two thirds of users visit business pages weekly (Bassig, 2021a).

- While 55% see Facebook as a prime platform for discovering new brands, 66% likely to share their buying experiences (Bassig, 2021a).

What Are Facebook Reviews?

In 2018, Facebook business Page transitioned to *Facebook Recommendations*. They now adopt a "Yes" or "No" system like Netflix and YouTube.

Users can now recommend a business by responding to a query in the "Recommendations" and "Reviews" section. They can also add extra details with tags, images, and text. But local business owners will no longer see star-based reviews. Furthermore, customers now assess businesses through recommendations.

Now you understand what Facebook reviews are, why is it important?

Why Are Facebook Reviews Important?

Facebook reviews are crucial for a brand's marketing strategy, with 92.4% of shoppers relying on them (Bassig, 2022). These reviews offer social validation and help people decide whether to buy from a company. As such, use Facebook reviews to improve user experience, outshine competitors, and attract more clients.

You may wonder how you'll know your Facebook reviews. So let's talk about it next.

Where Can You Find Your Business's Facebook Reviews?

Click the "Recommendations" tab under your profile photo to view your business feedback. You can filter them by "Most Recent" or "Most Helpful."

All evaluations and recommendations are public. Thus, your page visitors will see them. If you're curious about how you get your business rating, Facebook uses your past reviews and "Yes" or "No" recommendations.

You should respond to your Facebook reviews now that you've read them. But how?

How Can You Interact With a Facebook Reviewer?

Facebook endorsements and reviews appear under "Reviews." Thus, you can engage with your reviewers through comments, likes, or loves. But remember to use your business account for interactions and learn to address negative and positive comments.

Among consumers, 44.6% are likely to patronize a company if it replies to negative reviews, with 53.3% expecting a response within a week (Bassig, 2022). With many customers drawn to companies responding to negative feedback, ensure you deal with them immediately.

You should handle criticism and compliments because they affect your brand's success. But learn to choose the right words to set you apart from competitors. Also, encourage customer recommendations on Facebook to boost visibility and credibility.

How Can You Ask Customers to Give a Facebook Recommendation?

After obtaining consent, you can request reviews on your Facebook Page by sending customized SMS or emails to clients. Also, ensure to offer tangible reminders at busy spots for in-person visitors.

Keep a concise and friendly approach. You should explain the importance of feedback to your customers. Remember to provide a short link for easy submission.

Besides Facebook, encourage Google reviews, as 87% of consumers used Google to assess local businesses in 2021 (Paget, 2023).

What You Should Know About Google Reviews

Consumers seek trusted businesses and rely on recommendations and online reviews. It's especially true for expensive or risky products. In recent times, Google reviews have become vital to purchasing. When searching for local businesses, 76% of consumers regularly check them (Paget, 2023).

What Are Google Reviews for Businesses?

Google reviews for businesses appear prominently on search engine results pages (SERPs). Thus, they influence potential clients.

You must maintain a top-ranked Google Business Profile if you want more customers. Ensure your business has a strong reputation, including 5-star ratings. You'll boost your visual presence on Google if you do.

Why Are Google Reviews Important?

Local businesses depend on online reviews for customer decisions. A survey reported that 92% avoid companies with negative feedback. At the same time, 79% trust reviews as personal recommendations (Paget, 2023).

Google Business Profile ratings heavily influence searchers' opinions and purchases. Such reviews affect local rankings, including Google Local Pack, Local Finder, and organic rankings. Also, their value is consistently increasing.

To stay in the game, encourage satisfied customers to provide positive feedback on your Google Business Profile.

Where Can You Find Your Business Profile's Google Reviews?

There are three methods to handle reviews on your Business Profile:

Use Google Search

Search your business name on Google to read your reviews. Use the Business Profile Manager panel to access your profile. Then, click on Customers, then Reviews, to manage customer feedback.

Use Google Maps App

Access your Business Profile on mobile via the Google Maps app by tapping the account menu. Then, tap "Customers and Reviews" to view all reviews. Remember to use your Business Profile email for Google search or Maps app.

Use Business Profile Manager

Sign in to your Business Profile Manager to read customer feedback. Select the business profile you wish to check and then click on "Reviews."

How Can You Interact With Your Google Reviewer?

BrightLocal says 20% expect a response within a day (Paget, 2023). Thus, strive to respond immediately to customer reviews on Google. Also, you should always be polite when communicating with your reviewers.

You should address negative reviews because they offer valuable feedback for improvement. Also, handling them can turn unsatisfied customers into satisfied ones.

How to Reply to Negative Feedback

When facing a negative review, stay composed and respond politely. You should thank the customer and apologize if needed. Then, briefly explain if factors were beyond your control and invite the customer for an offline discussion.

Also, you must avoid sharing personal details or attacking the reviewer. Instead, focus on demonstrating your obligation to ensure customer happiness. Remember, readers can usually identify difficult-to-please individuals and understand occasional negative feedback.

How Can You Ask Your Customers to Give Google Reviews?

Obtaining reviews is crucial for local businesses. Thus, you should encourage satisfied customers to provide feedback. Check these tips on asking for Google reviews.

Use the Business Profile Review Form

First, give a short URL for your Business Profile review form, and ask customers for feedback. You can also include the URL in feedback cards, email signatures, receipts, or your website.

Use the Google Maps App

Second, in the Maps app, find your business and select "Share Profile" in the "Get More Reviews" panel for a short review URL. Remember to get permission from your customers before sharing via text or email.

Use Business Profile Manager

Third, manage several profiles by signing in to Business Profile Manager and selecting the desired company for a short review URL. Click "Get More Reviews" and "Share Review." Remember, you can't offer bribes or incentives. Also, avoid setting up a review station as they violate Google review policies. If a review violates any Google policies, you must report it for removal.

Facebook and Google aren't the only platforms offering reviews. If you want to generate more customer reviews, why don't you try YouTube too?

Why You Should Use YouTube to Gather Customer Reviews

YouTube videos accumulate over a billion views daily. Thus, the online video-sharing app is the perfect platform for obtaining customer feedback. Client reviews offer valuable advantages for consumers and businesses for five reasons:

YouTube Generates More Engagement

First, video content boosts online engagement by 94% (Hollingsworth, 2023). Thus, making customer video testimonials is more impactful than text reviews. You can encourage YouTube video sharing for greater brand visibility. If you encounter negative feedback, you must address it promptly to enhance customer loyalty and Net Promoter Score.

Create a YouTube business channel for your customers to share their reviews. If it becomes successful, it can increase engagement. You may achieve a higher success rate in this video-sharing platform than in customer surveys.

People Trust and Can Relate to YouTube Influencers

Second, YouTube, a reliable platform for how-to guides and product reviews, fosters high trust among users. Many customers consult YouTube before buying products, with 42% viewing it as the most trustworthy source (Adewolu, 2015).

YouTube Videos Are Shareable and Intelligible

Third, videos provide an easy and captivating method for sharing content online. You can use them, especially for collecting client feedback. Utilizing platforms like YouTube allows effortless collection and response to user opinions.

Positive feedback can serve as testimonials. At the same time, negative feedback helps identify and address problem areas.

Videos Are More Engaging

Fourth, video feedback channels gain a significant boost in response rates. They now offer a cost-efficient alternative to focus groups and survey promotions.

Video Streaming Is the Trend

Fifth, video content is on the rise, embraced by major social media platforms. It's now a leader in views, engagement, and improved search rankings. You must embrace this trend to become a market leader and use technology to efficiently gather insights from review videos. If you do so, you ensure customer satisfaction and loyalty.

Facebook, Google, and YouTube are essential review platforms, but we must discuss another to complete the big four. You'll learn more about Yelp next.

Why You Should Use Yelp to Gather Customer Reviews

Yelp is a popular online platform. It specializes in customer reviews and business recommendations across various industries. You can use it to gather customer reviews to generate many business advantages.

Here are some reasons you should use Yelp for collecting customer reviews:

Established Reputation

Yelp has built a reputation as a trusted source for customer reviews. Many consumers turn to it when buying. They get insights from customers who have used a particular brand or service. By leveraging its credibility, you can gain your potential customer's trust. Moreover, you can enhance your business reputation.

Large User Base

Yelp boasts millions of active monthly visitors who seek information and reviews. This broad reach allows you to tap into a vast audience and increase your brand exposure. Also, positive reviews on Yelp can attract new customers.

Enhanced Business Visibility

Yelp's search functionality and integration with search engines increase your company's online visibility. Customers can find your business because Yelp listings often appear in search results. Your brand lands on top of the search results if it has high ratings and positive reviews. Moreover, it can attract organic traffic to your company website.

Engaged Community

Yelp promotes an engaged community of users. Active members can share their opinions, experiences, and recommendations on the platform. You can use it to encourage satisfied customers to leave reviews.

As you already know, positive reviews attract new customers and can generate buzz for your brand. They also help your business establish itself as reputable and reliable.

Consumer Insights

Yelp provides valuable insights into customer preferences, feedback, and trends. You can gain insights into what aspects of your business resonate with customers. Moreover, you can identify areas for improvement through the platform. These insights can inform business decisions, enhance customer experiences, and drive growth.

Facebook, Google, YouTube, and Yelp are the top platforms you can use for collecting customer reviews, but they can be cumbersome. Can you improve the process of generating customer feedback?

Making it Easy: Sharing Links and Simplifying the Process

Collecting customer reviews can take time and effort. Thus, strive to simplify the process. But how?

How to Simplify the Customer Reviews

Focus on customer centricity in your dynamic product development by incorporating user feedback. This approach enhances customer experience, uncovers valuable insights, and boosts sales.

Here are five ways to simplify user feedback:

Collect Reviews Correctly

First, streamline user feedback collection by choosing efficient methods for each customer group. For example, pick in-app surveys for new users and personalized calls for active members. For initial product development stages, you can use focus groups.

Proactively gather feedback via surveys, usability tests, and direct communication. Remember to balance frequency to avoid overloading customers.

Analyze the Data

Second, not all feedback is equally valuable. Focus on active users familiar with your product's development. Categorize feedback according to business goals, and use sentimental analysis for context. It helps to understand customer preferences and enables quick responses via social media.

Ensure you implement a structured system for organizing feedback to gain insights.

Consolidate Your Customer Feedback Journey

Third, optimize user feedback from collection to implementation to reduce confusion and inefficiency. At the same time, optimization saves development resources.

Track Customer Reviews

Fourth, gather and segment user feedback, then develop a prioritized task list for your team. Use an app to rank requests according to business objectives, customer value, and lifecycle stages. Use metrics suitable for your industry and audience. Also, streamline conversions, reduce support costs, and simplify sales.

Listen to Your Customers

Fifth, close the loop with survey participants and use follow-up questions. Share feedback through personalized emails and community posts. Doing so can help strengthen relationships and build trust.

You should streamline the feedback process and enhance review collection efforts. But you can't do everything by yourself. Involve your employees, especially those interacting with customers frequently.

Employee Advocacy: Encouraging Staff to Ask for Reviews

Online reviews are vital. Involving your staff is crucial as they represent your business and interact with customers daily. Engage them in your review-building strategy to see growth in reviews.

How to Encourage Your Employees to Collect Customer Reviews

Finding a solution for your business can be frustrating if you have unsupportive employees. As a business owner, overcome this challenge using strategies to empower your staff to collect customer reviews.

Gain the support of your team with these techniques:

Provide a Reward

First, reward top review-collecting employees for motivating and encouraging friendly competition. For example, consider team competitions, offering prizes like gift cards or lunches. Seek input on preferred rewards. But ensure staff follows guidelines to protect the company's reputation.

Ask Your Employees to Help

Second, request your team's help in obtaining online reviews. You should emphasize their significance to your business.

Provide a Script

Third, share successful customer interaction examples with your team. For instance, use a script requesting online reviews from satisfied clients. But adapt the dialogue to suit your business and assist employees in connecting with customers.

Acknowledge Employee Mentioned in the Customer Review

Fourth, reward employees mentioned in reviews, encouraging them to build strong customer relationships. Identify the employee based on customer experience and description, even if not explicitly named.

How I Increased Google Customer Reviews for One of My Consulting Clients

I want to share the technique I discovered which is effective in boosting customer reviews from Google. I asked my consulting client to prepare postcards with a QR code for their staff to give to their customers at the end of their visits. The consulting client's employees ask them to leave an honest review if they liked their service.

If the business received a less-than-perfect review, another team member quickly replied to ask about the customer's experience. If they couldn't immediately resolve the issue, the client ensured that they had time to contact their customer to ask how they could make up for it.

My consulting client listens to every complaint for their business to improve. Fortunately, they only have handled a few customer problems. Everyone on my client's team understands the value of satisfying their clients.

This step discussed generating customer reviews from Facebook, Google, and YouTube. You learned how to encourage your staff to seek customer feedback. It's challenging but rewarding as well.

Facebook, Google, and YouTube aren't the only platforms where you can engage your customers to ask for reviews. You should use every opportunity to rake in feedback. The next step will tell you how.

Chapter 7:

Step 5—Ask for Reviews

Wonder what customers really want? Ask. Don't tell. –Lisa Stone

Requesting reviews is vital in attracting more clients and establishing a solid online presence. This step underscores the significance of favorable testimonials. It also offers practical advice on soliciting customer feedback through various means.

Furthermore, the step highlights ideal approaches for seeking reviews. Such techniques can enhance your digital reputation, client confidence, and allegiance. As a result, your business also generates increased income.

Before we discuss the strategies, let's first learn the importance of asking for reviews.

Why You Should Ask for Reviews

Undoubtedly, customer testimonials significantly influence purchasing decisions. Opinions from others about your product have more priority than your statements, even if they come from total strangers. Do you still need convincing? Look at these online review statistics:

- Internet testimonials are relied upon by 84% of buyers as much as they rely on personal recommendations (Courvoisier, 2019).

- Enhancing your review star rating by 1.5 could result in an additional 13,000 leads (Donahue, 2018).

If you still want more proof before you consider asking for reviews, consider the following statistics:

- Customers are open to it. Research by BrightLocal revealed that 76% of individuals invited to submit reviews follow through (Paget, 2023).

- Customers find reviews useful. According to a Podium study, 93% of consumers believe a local business's online reviews are as vital as Amazon product reviews (Podium, 2017).

- Customers actively search for reviews. BrightLocal says 98% of customers read online reviews for domestic businesses (Marchant, 2017).

The stats prove the significance of reviews. Thus, you should plan on acquiring them from your customers. But how? The next topic will help you.

How to Ask for Reviews

You must increase your Google feedback and enhance your Yelp scores. You must also boost your YouTube reviews and Facebook recommendations. Here are several methods to request them:

- face-to-face

- by phone

- through text

- on your website (preferably on a "Reviews" page)

- through email (mass email, individual email, business email, email signatures)

- using social media (private messages or posts)

- on thank-you cards

- on receipts or invoices

In this section, we'll discuss all these methods. But remember, you can always use a combination of strategies to ask clients for feedback. Implement several concurrent tactics to ensure you receive consistent comments about your company.

Many up-to-date reviews can help your business rank higher in search results and increase customer trust.

Before you begin, verify that your company's information is accurate on platforms like Google, Bing, and others.

Ask for Reviews in Person

Requesting a review face-to-face might seem daunting, but it's the most successful method. Take advantage of any opportunities that arise!

The most straightforward situation is when a customer gives you unsolicited compliments. In this instance, show gratitude for their feedback and propose the idea.

Requesting a review doesn't have to be a waiting game. But you'll need to engage your customers more often in a conversation presenting the opportunity. Upon checkout, ask about their experience with your products, services, or store.

Wait to ask for a review after a customer's first positive comment about your business. It can make the conversation seem insincere if you ask at the first instance. Your client may think you only care about obtaining the review.

Although reviews enhance your reputation, if you don't do it right, it can lead to no feedback and a damaged reputation. Instead, gauge the customer's mood. If their answer is brief and suggests they don't want to chat, don't push them.

If they reply positively and provide more feedback or information, continue the discussion. When the communication comes to an end, ask for a review.

Ask for Reviews Over the Phone

Many opportunities arise for you to request client reviews via phone. But be selective in whom you approach for feedback. It's best to avoid asking clients who have just experienced a lengthy or challenging issue. But if a customer openly expresses satisfaction and gratitude for your help, consider it the best time to request feedback.

Ask for Reviews Through Text

With the rise of voice dictation typing and short reviews, consumers can now easily interact with brands. They can also post reviews directly from their smartphones or tablets.

If you send customers a review invitation through SMS, you boost the likelihood that they'll click the link. Text messages are more likely to be opened by 98% of people compared to emails (Shibu, 2020).

Also, further studies reveal that people read 90% of SMS within the first 3 minutes (Mobilesquared, 2010). Thus, you should design an effective SMS review request. Remember, text messages may have character restrictions.

Ask for Reviews on Your Website

Incorporate a call to action (CTA) for submitting reviews in different areas of your website. But consider having a specific "Reviews" or "Testimonials" page accessible through the menu. Potential customers often search for this feature when evaluating a company.

Create a "Submit Your Review" Page

Your website can feature a review section in your main navigation, allowing users to read and submit reviews. Users can approve or disapprove on the "Submit a Review" page. After selecting thumbs up, they can also leave a Google review.

Display Existing Reviews

Ensure there is a page displaying current reviews, or incorporate them directly onto your "Submit a Review" page. It demonstrates the brevity of reviews and offers a starting point for users.

Many content management systems provide scripts or plug-ins to collect your customer feedback from several platforms into this page's feed. Alternatively, you can add them manually.

Regardless of the method, display the reviews as text (rather than screenshots or images). Reviews often contain crucial keywords enhancing your SEO. Thus, Google won't recognize these words if they're in the pictures.

Ask for Reviews Through Email

Email is one of the most efficient methods to request customer feedback. It allows you to tailor your review inquiries to client loyalty and satisfaction while linking them to a recent transaction.

The email should direct customers to a platform where they can give their feedback. Keep your request brief and customized. Many clients favor providing their opinions via email. Thus, take excerpts from these messages, and feature them in promotional materials or on your website.

Ask for Reviews Using Social Media

Upon examining your social media profiles, you may discover the genuine responses your clients provide.

They give encouraging remarks in your post's comments, so begin exploring what these customers express.

When you come across a persuasive evaluation, contact the client. Request their consent to share the testimonial they have previously composed. It doesn't need extra work from the clients. Thus, they'll probably agree to your request to publish their feedback.

Also, it's readily accessible to your potential clients, albeit in a disordered fashion. Thus, you should gather these reviews systematically and seek their authorization.

Ask for Reviews on Thank-You Cards

Utilizing a design platform lets you craft small appreciation cards for your customers. You can include them in product packaging, attach to invoices, or place them beside mints that prompt feedback. The card could display messages such as:

- "Were you satisfied with our collaboration? Please leave a review!"

- "How was your encounter with us? Share your thoughts by posting a review at [link]!"

- "Have any comments? We're happy to receive them! Please submit a review at [link]."

Ask for Reviews in Receipts or Invoices

You may need more time frequently interacting with clients and using an email list. In that case, you can request feedback at the end of your receipts.

Configure your device to add a brief note at the end of each invoice. It can feature your Google review link or any other platform where you'd like to receive more testimonials. Consider using one of these phrases:

- Please share your experience with us [insert link].

- Express your support [insert link].

- Have you enjoyed your time here? Please give us a review [insert link]!

- Local backing keeps us thriving. Provide feedback here [insert link].

- Support community businesses. Submit a review here [insert link].

- Please tell others about us and leave us a review [insert link].

- Assist others in discovering us. Post a review here [insert link].

Aside from asking for customer feedback through your website and social media pages, ask for reviews on review websites. You'll learn how next.

How to Request Feedback on Review Sites

Inform your customers if you wish to expand your brand's visibility on particular review platforms. For instance, a hotel chain might have good reviews on Tripadvisor but could use more on Google or Facebook. Read the recommendations and top strategies for asking for customer feedback on specific sites.

Ask for Google Reviews

Online Review Statistics discovered that Google surpasses other review platforms on online reviews. As a result, seeking Google reviews from customers has become a preferred marketing tactic. Here are some valuable suggestions for obtaining Google reviews.

Establish a Google Business Review Link

By generating a specific link and sharing it with your customers, you motivate them to review your business on Google.

After obtaining your Google review link, you can share it on your email campaigns and social media networks. You can also use it on printed receipts, customer feedback forms, or in any other situation where customers might leave a review.

Use Google Review Stickers

Another straightforward method to get more Google reviews is through Google review stickers. You can find these stickers in the Google Business Profile marketing kit. This tool can help you to produce, download, and print personalized promotional materials.

Also, you can convert your feedback and business information into social posts, stickers, and posters. The content of these materials primarily focuses on promoting your business through testimonials. It also encourages customers to find your business on Google and share their images and reviews.

Once listed, you can access a page containing your personalized "Review Us on Google" marketing kit. It includes posters, window stickers, table tents, social media posts, and other creative resources.

You can request these materials by mail or download them for convenient printing and sharing. If your business isn't on Google, you can begin by claiming your business listings through Google Business Profile. A local listing management solution may suit larger companies with many locations.

Establish Your Company's Presence on Yelp

Yelp's guidelines on reviews and content disallow companies from requesting customer feedback. But you can enhance your company's presence on Yelp and actively interact with its users.

Follow these tips to boost Yelp visibility:

- Inform your audience that they can locate your business on Yelp.

- Include links to your Yelp business pages in emails, newsletters, and printed materials.

- Get Yelp stickers and display these promotional items at your business sites.

Ask for Tripadvisor Reviews

Unlike Yelp, Tripadvisor permits businesses to request reviews. The travel website offers free tools to boost your brand's visibility on the platform. Moreover, it helps generate more reviews. For instance, Tripadvisor stickers can increase traffic and conversions. At the same time, they promote reviews on the site. Most listings on the website qualify for a standard collection of Tripadvisor stickers. Here are some examples:

- "Operating Hours"

- "Complimentary Wi-Fi"

- "Provide Us With a Tripadvisor Review" or "Leave a Review for Us on Tripadvisor"

Some listings may also be eligible for other stickers, such as the following:

- "Reserve With Us on Tripadvisor"

- "Featured, Rated, or Suggested on Tripadvisor"

- "Certificate of Excellence recognition"

Now you know how to request reviews, you should understand what to avoid when requesting feedback.

Things You Can't Do When Asking for Reviews

You already know the proper technique to request reviews. Now, let's examine a few tactics to avoid when planning to enhance your internet testimonials.

Don't Offer Incentives

Under no conditions should you provide a discount or complimentary item for submitting reviews if it violates terms of service of the review platform. It may result in poor-quality or textless star-only reviews.

The primary goal of feedback is not to promote the business. It's to enable potential clients to make knowledgeable choices.

Don't Buy Reviews

Avoid purchasing counterfeit evaluations! Sophisticated review platforms use several methods to identify deceptive actions about online feedback. Be cautious about penalties or your company's removal from the site due to such conduct!

Don't Be Shy to Ask for Reviews

Individuals are typically open to providing their opinions. They enjoy expressing themselves and are more likely to support a business that has fulfilled their needs as a form of reciprocation. Furthermore, you enable them to assist similar customers in confidently making educated choices.

Don't Annoy Your Clients for Reviews

Continuously bombarding your devoted clients with excessive requests for reviews can irritate them. If you persistently seek feedback, customers may provide negative or unsuitable reviews. It could even transform a satisfied customer into a displeased one.

Don't Ask for a Specific Review

It's always beneficial to simplify the process for clients to submit feedback. You can offer examples and guidelines to spark their creativity. But requesting a particularly favorable review or a 5-star rating is inadvisable. Furthermore, refrain from asking customers to delete any negative evaluations.

Remember to Reply to Reviews

At the onset, this method signifies recognition and gratitude for the clients' efforts in taking the time to engage. Next, it aids in fostering customer connections and increasing retention rates. Lastly, it demonstrates to the broader audience that you pay close attention to your customer's feedback. Also, replying promotes interaction and involvement in your listing. Google considers these factors when determining the rank of business listings.

When You Should Ask for Reviews

When aiming to get more feedback, it's crucial to decide on the ideal time to request customer feedback. An analysis of over 150,000 reviews by ReviewTrackers (2021) reveals the following:

- The optimal time frame for requesting reviews is between 12 p.m. and 7 p.m.

- The best times to request feedback are 2–3 p.m. and 6–7 p.m. Customers will most likely use Google to rate a business during these periods.

Individuals frequently visit businesses during lunch breaks or after work. Thus, these hours are prime for consumers to reflect on their experiences.

- When should you avoid asking for reviews? According to data from ReviewTrackers, few people write reviews between 2 a.m. and 3 a.m. Also, review generation is slow from when individuals wake up (approximately 6–7 a.m.) until lunch (around 12–1 p.m.).

These findings should help you plan effectively. It's always best to check, analyze, and update. Know the perfect times to send review requests to generate the most feedback.

Sample: Email Template for Asking for Reviews

"Hello all!

Great feedback from amazing clients like yourself allows others to trust [business name]. Please visit [link to review platform] and express your delightful experiences. We will be eternally thankful.

We appreciate your help in advance!"

Client testimonials are influential resources for establishing credibility and enhancing your promotional endeavors. They hold significant sway over potential customers' buying choices. Also, they help achieve your business objectives. You can clearly understand requesting client feedback and transforming ideas into reality.

Apply the knowledge earned and focus on top-performing strategies. It will cause a constant flow of favorable client evaluations. Also, you can outsmart your competition, especially if they need to know more about the initial steps of soliciting feedback.

But after collecting reviews, what should you do next? You use social media to share customer experiences.

Chapter 8:

Step 6—Share Customer Experiences on Your Social Media Accounts

Social media is not a media. The key is to listen, engage, and build relationships. –David Alston

Promoting client interactions on social media platforms can contribute to a company's expansion. It can enhance its internet presence and foster confidence among prospective customers. Also, it can cultivate a sense of camaraderie surrounding the brand.

By emphasizing customer reviews and input, you can connect with your audience. Also, it can prove the worth your business delivers. Social networks like Instagram, Twitter, and Facebook provide various tools and options. They can simplify sharing customer experiences and reactions. Thus, a social media marketing strategy allows you to gain and keep customers.

Before we get into the details, let's first discuss the reasons for using social media to promote positive reviews of your business.

Why Use Social Media to Promote Customer Feedback

Social media usage continues to grow, with a 10.1% increase in users from 2021 to 2022, adding 424 million new users. Now, 58.4% of the global population (4.62 billion people) actively uses social media for 147 minutes daily. The usage totals 53,655 minutes every year (DataReportal, 2023).

Despite the negative publicity, users continue engaging with platforms. More often, they seek feedback on a product they want to buy. Considering the vast audience, social sharing of customer reviews would be ideal.

The ReviewTrackers (2022a) report revealed key insights:

- Google dominates as the top review platform.

- Review interactions have surged 50% since pre-pandemic levels.

- Within a week, 53% of consumers expect businesses to tackle negative feedback.

- Swift review responses are crucial for upholding a positive reputation.

These stats prove that social media has become a prevalent way of sharing customer reviews. As an entrepreneur, will you not use it to benefit your business?

What Your Brand Will Gain From Social Media Testimonials

Social media enables companies and influencers to influence their audience and promote offerings. You can effectively navigate this platform by leveraging customer feedback and endorsements. You can also boost conversion rates and involvement.

Testimonials and client evaluations enhance your brand's social credibility through the following:

Establish Trust

First, genuine customer feedback and experiences are free from marketing tactics. They can boost confidence in your brand and offerings among social media followers.

Speed Up Sales Conversions

Second, prospective customers hesitate to purchase online. This hesitancy stems from their inability to examine products or services personally. Customer testimonials help overcome this barrier, simplifying decision-making.

As a powerful social media tool, testimonials boost sales conversion rates. They add credibility and a personal touch to your brand.

Establish a Proper Customer Expectation

Third, customer experiences should align more with online expectations. Reviews and testimonials provide authentic insights and firsthand feedback. They help reduce uncertainty and improve service representation.

Knowing the benefits of sharing customer reviews on social media is a good way of understanding the concept. But how do you go about it?

Ingenious Ways of Sharing Client Feedback on Social Media

We examined the benefits of sharing customer feedback on social media and where to get it. But simply requesting and posting testimonials is insufficient. Ensure your hard-earned testimonials generate the attention they deserve.

To address this opportunity, here are six inventive methods to showcase your customer reviews on social media. Using these suggestions can turn your brand's customer testimonials into influential assets.

Interviews

First, engage on social media through story-driven dialogues and interview-style client feedback. This approach keeps content concise. It can also effectively communicate critical business information while avoiding overly scripted interactions.

Here are some methods to showcase customer reviews in this manner:

- Choose comfortable, regular customers with previous reviews for video or audio testimonials.

Ask relevant questions through text overlays or voice-overs.

- For camera-shy customers, use animation and graphic design in a question and answer format, with bonus points for voice-overs.

- Engage non-reviewed clients with questionnaires. Also, try to repurpose responses into social media videos or carousel posts. Remember, video and audio quality are crucial for success.

Ensure your customers record their videos with ample lighting. There shouldn't be noise interference too. Reviewers should look professional, and use a high-quality microphone. If you'll be present for the recording, bring a ring light and interview in a soundproof room.

Video Testimonials

Second, brief reviews and customer interactions may need more information for interview-style formats. Sometimes, pursuing clients for detailed reviews is impractical. But video testimonials excel on social media.

Maximize the video potential by enhancing short testimonials. Remember to use introductions, product footage, text overlays, and closing frames. For maximum impact and enjoyability, ensure you create engaging content.

Also, you can combine client videos of the same product or service for promotion to boost engagement on social media platforms. But know each platform's specific requirements before uploading them for optimal performance.

Social Media Ads

Third, social proof significantly impacts sales by boosting conversions and building trust. Incorporate customer feedback into digital ads and landing pages to highlight your brand's value.

Remember to include testimonials in promotional videos for specific products or services. Also, you should optimize video ads for social platforms. Ensure you use text overlays and closed captions.

Stories and Feed Posts

Fourth, use client testimonials on your social media channels and Stories. They can prove your customers' satisfaction with your business. Consider initiating a weekly segment where you share customer feedback. For your feed, include the following:

- Google Business Profile evaluations

- Facebook business Page ratings

- survey responses

- email feedback

- third-party platform appraisals

When sharing these reviews on your social media feed, feature a photo, name, and the reviewed product. But merely sharing these won't suffice, so enhance them through the following:

- Extract an interesting quote from the review. Then, include your company's logo, product image, and customer details to transform it into a branded graphic design post.

- Use an audio recording to produce an audiogram.

- Implement attention-grabbing headlines before sharing the review. It will encourage customers to engage more with the content.

Apply design elements to Stories, repost positive mentions, and create highlights for easy access. Use visual content like images and videos for better social media performance. Collaborate with professionals for branded graphics and videos aligned with your brand identity.

Customer Journey Feature

Fifth, showcasing client testimonials is a powerful approach for enterprises. It primarily benefits beauty businesses, fitness centers, and healthcare providers. You can extract stories to feature character growth, motivation, and genuine transformation.

For example, you can show before and after pictures on your website if you're a fitness center owner. Including customer emotions and your role in their experience creates highly impactful content.

This method showcases your work effectively with the option to use photos or videos for customer journeys. Use videos to engage viewers and increase time spent on your social media. They help boost visibility and message delivery to your target audience.

GIFs

Sixth, showcase customer feedback on social media using popular and shareable GIFs. Personalized GIFs with customer images and quotes offer a playful yet professional approach. They convey information in a compact format. GIFs in campaigns have been successful because animations make testimonials eye-catching and engaging.

To ensure high-quality visuals, request high-resolution pictures from clients. Use them for your testimonial and review posts. Such a strategy will result in impressive custom GIFs and other post types. Ultimately, you're able to boost brand awareness with them.

Use these top strategies to share customer feedback on social media. But if you have a specific platform in mind, you can check the ideas for boosting and sharing customer feedback.

Inspiring Ideas on Sharing Customer Feedback on Social Media

A strong endorsement can effectively prove your worth and skills to your target audience. Still, acting quickly for maximum effect is crucial when showcasing them on social media.

Fortunately, there are several excellent methods to enhance your testimonials by making them more captivating and eye-catching and more enduring.

Check the following suggestions for encouragement to use testimonials on social media platforms.

How to Share Customer Reviews on Instagram

Instagram Stories compress your testimonials into easily understandable and swiftly consumable content. They're concise and influential social proof.

Stories stand out due to their vertical format. While most online content (except for TikTok and Snapchat) is horizontal or square, Stories break the norm.

Here are various ways to share your testimonial on Stories:

- Rather than merely copying and pasting text into a Story, design a template to craft visually appealing testimonials.

- Use built-in platform features to make your testimonial distinctive and engaging.

How to Share Customer Reviews on Facebook

Facebook offers less personalization than Instagram. But you can use many methods to show your testimonials creatively.

Video and imaginative design can transform an actual testimonial into something more engaging. Even if you can't get a video testimonial, you can still display it in a visually appealing manner instead of just a text post.

How to Share Customer Reviews on Twitter

Brevity and rapidity are essential as content moves swiftly! To leave a mark with your shared material,

- maintain concise and captivating testimonials

- incorporate visuals to occupy more room on users' feeds

- use them to emphasize crucial terms and convey necessary information

How to Share Customer Reviews on LinkedIn

LinkedIn offers an ideal platform to display endorsements through various content types. Use it to share videos, images, text posts, articles, PDFs, and slideshows.

While there's no limit to sharing endorsements on LinkedIn, avoid sales pitches and boasting. Focus on expressing gratitude and highlighting client success. Remember to use creative formats to make your content visually appealing.

Use these concepts to promote customer reviews on your social media accounts. Finally, check the best practices for sharing customer feedback to propel your business upward.

Best Practices for Promoting Customer Feedback on Social Media

After getting customer testimonials from several sources, spread the positive word to your audience. Below are five strategies for showcasing your client's feedback on social media:

Opt for a Short Message

First, avoid sharing a complete customer testimonial on social media platforms. Instead, select a crucial part and use it as an eye-catching title. Following that, if relevant, you can provide a link to the entire review within the content of your social media update.

Use Visuals

Second, use visuals to engage social media audiences with customer feedback. Use short, vertical video testimonials for multi-platform use, or share review screenshots. Create custom-branded content with crucial quotes from in-depth reviews.

Remember to Thank Your Clients

Third, thank your customers. Are you looking to motivate more clients to provide their thoughts on your customer's product or service? You must express your gratitude to clients for investing their time in offering their opinions. A basic "thank you" shows that you have read and valued every piece of feedback obtained.

Share Customer Feedback

Fourth, track your social media accounts for customer praise, and repost them for increased visibility. Retweet on Twitter, but get written consent for Instagram and Facebook Feed shares.

Use Instagram Stories to reshare customer testimonials. Ensure you include user posts, as they'll link to the original. Share mentions in Stories, incorporating mentioned content in your own Story and crediting the actual user.

Optimize Cross-Promotion With a Content Calendar

Fifth, maintaining a balance in your social media calendar is essential. Avoid overusing testimonials to prevent appearing self-absorbed and repelling potential clients.

Remember to include client feedback alongside other materials to reinforce core campaign messages. Combine scheduled content with reshares and spontaneous thank-you messages. Ensure you have the appropriate mix and tone for maximum benefit.

Since most people use social media nowadays, you must establish your business presence on these networks. Instead of plain text, try to animate your posts using visuals and ads. Using social media, you can boost your trustworthiness and sales conversions and set expectations.

But using customer feedback on social media is only part of the process. You can't share something you don't have. Thus, encourage your customers to leave more reviews you can share on your social media account. We'll discuss this step in detail next.

Chapter 9:

Step 7—Encourage Customers to Leave Reviews

Call it what you will, incentives are what get people to work harder. –Nikita Khrushchev

You can increase review volume and improve your online reputation. You can do so by offering incentives for feedback and promoting positive experiences on company-owned platforms and social media. However, be careful about providing a reward or incentive for customer reviews on third-party review sites because most platforms don't allow incentivizing feedback.

Listening and making improvements based on reviews enhances customer experiences. They also lead to more positive feedback and business growth. This step will discuss ways to invite your clients to leave reviews.

Creating Incentives: Review Terms of Service and Encouraging Feedback

Consumers increasingly rely on reviews during their online shopping experience. Recent research shows 99.9% of consumers read reviews, up from 97% in 2018. Ideally, customers look for products with 26 or more reviews. Nearly a third prefer 100 or more testimonials (PowerReviews, 2021). But how can you incentivize customer feedback?

How Do You Persuade Customers to Leave Reviews?

While only some customers write glowing reviews, research shows 52% of consumers create feedback many times monthly. At the same time, the rest submit less frequently or never (Smith, 2021).

To increase review volume, offering incentives is highly effective. The proof is that 73% of consumers would write reviews if incentivized. This strategy appeals to shoppers across all generations (Smith, 2021). But what incentives can you give your customers to write reviews?

Effective Incentives That Generate Reviews

A recent survey of more than 10,000 consumers revealed four top incentives for writing reviews. Explore these alternatives to discover the most suitable for your brand.

Free Products

People love free stuff. Offering free products is a highly effective way to generate reviews. A survey found that 91% of consumers wrote a product review because of the freebie. Also, sending free samples for reviews has an average 85% submission rate and results in higher-quality feedback. These detailed reviews are essential to 56% of consumers. Thus, product sampling is a valuable strategy for increasing review volume and quality (Smith, 2021).

Get a Product Before Its Launch

Early access to products gives customers a sense of exclusivity and encourages them to write reviews.

According to a survey, 85% of consumers will write a review for prelaunch products. Thus, this strategy can help gather valuable feedback and build a solid review base (Smith, 2021).

Use prelaunch reviews to identify product strengths and weaknesses. Do it before the official release so you have time for the improvements.

Offer Brand or Store Discounts

Consumers actively seek deals and discounts, with 72% using coupons to save money (Gaffney, 2020). Offering discounts can encourage 67% of shoppers to write reviews (PowerReviews, 2021).

Consider providing deals, such as a percentage off or free shipping on future purchases. Do so in exchange for submitting a review. Offering discounts or deals can boost reviews and encourage repeat purchases. Due to coupons, 54% of consumers admit buying on impulse (Gaffney, 2020).

Offer Brand or Store Loyalty Points

Brand loyalty is significant. Emotionally connected customers stay for 5.1 years and have a 306% higher lifetime value (Tolliver-Walker, 2020).

Offering loyalty points in exchange for reviews can increase engagement and boost conversions. According to a survey, 59% of consumers say they can write reviews for loyalty points (PowerReviews, 2021).

Use your existing loyalty program to boost reviews. You can offer customers points for each review. They can then exchange these points for promotions or discounts on future purchases.

Inform Your Customer About Your Incentives

You've selected an incentive to encourage customer reviews—great! Now, inform customers about it. Most consumers need a reminder, like a post-purchase email, to write reviews. Such emails result in 80% of reviews (PowerReviews, 2021).

Prominently feature the incentive in your post-purchase emails, ideally at the top. This way, shoppers notice it even without scrolling. Additionally, consider including promotions in your packaging.

Tell Your Customers If It's an Incentivized Review

Consumers trust reviews as they come from genuine experiences. To maintain this trust, ensure transparency by indicating if a reviewer received incentives. This way, you also inform future shoppers.

If you want to increase your customer reviews, don't hesitate to provide incentives. But you should be transparent. State in the review section if a customer received incentives. Once you generate more reviews, you can use them to improve your product or service and business.

Using Reviews as a Tool for Improvement

Customer reviews are essential for enhancing your business and customer experience. They help identify customer needs. Also, they highlight improvement areas, like customer service or accurate quotes.

Understanding customer expectations leads to better operations, loyal clients, and effective marketing campaigns. Use reviews to refine, plan, and boost your online presence.

How Can Customer Reviews Help Improve Business Operations?

Customer reviews offer crucial insights into customer opinions, aiding business improvement. You can effectively address issues by identifying key areas such as service team performance or wait times.

Identify Business Key Areas to Improve

Negative customer feedback is inevitable. But you can use it to drive positive change in your business by identifying areas for improvement.

Search for Trends

Review customer feedback for recurring topics. Also, note the frequency of common complaints to identify prevalent issues.

Use Tools to Determine Recurring Themes

Streamline the review analysis process with an AI-powered tool. This way, you save time identifying keywords and trends in first- and third-party reviews. You can also use powerful filters to auto-tag content and uncover customers' critical reasons for praise or complaints.

Carry Out an Improvement Plan

Once you know which enhancements your customers want, develop a plan based on these insights.

Share the Reviews With Your Operations Staff

Multilocation businesses can assess service and product performance per location. For example, franchise grocery store branches may excel or need help with customer service. Based on customer reviews, adjusting staff schedules can address issues like long lines and slow service.

Share the Reviews With Your Business Development Staff

Customer reviews aid business development by improving offerings. They also help understand customer responses to pilots, services, new locations, or promotions.

Encourage Your Frontline Staff

Reviews are crucial for team improvement and motivation. Share positive feedback with team members to reinforce their efforts and show appreciation.

Use negative feedback to guide future training and resource allocation. This way, you ensure the team is well-prepared to address customer concerns.

Make Customers Feel Important

Customer reviews give you a way to appreciate customer feedback. Respond to positive and negative reviews thoughtfully. Also, appreciate customers' input, and outline its implementation in your business.

Regular clients value businesses adapting to their needs. At the same time, they provide valuable, in-depth reviews based on familiarity and experience.

Also, negative feedback turns positive when addressed and acted upon. It increases customer respect as businesses improve based on customer suggestions.

Include Customer Reviews in Your Marketing Plan

Customer reviews are a valuable evergreen marketing tool for your business. They show your advantages over competitors. Building a solid review collection requires effort and strategic use of marketing materials for the most impact.

Positive customer reviews are influential social proof, building trust in your business. These endorsements showcase your company, product, or service as excellent, satisfying previous customers.

Recent reviews on your website highlight your company as the best option for potential customers. Leverage reviews as social proof on Twitter, Facebook, and Instagram platforms. You can create visual quotes and incorporate them into email marketing campaigns.

Let's look at the success stories of companies using social networks for business growth.

Sharing Success Stories: Growing Your Business Through Social Media

Social media enables real-time customer interaction. It enhances reach, networking, and promotion of products or services. But be cautious and understand the pros and cons before beginning.

Advantages of Using Social Media for Business

Social media aids in customer engagement, feedback, and brand development. It enables businesses to expand market reach and reduces marketing costs. It also helps increase revenue through advertising and networking. Additionally, it assists in market research and staff recruitment. It also helps in website traffic growth and competitor monitoring.

Drawbacks of Using Social Media for Business

Social media may only suit some businesses. An unplanned social media presence can waste time and money.

Disadvantages include the following:

- need for extra resources

- daily monitoring

- potential unwanted behavior

- risk of negative feedback

- information leaks

- hacking

- false claims that are subject to consumer laws

Establish a social media strategy with policies and procedures beforehand to cut risks.

How to Craft a Social Media Strategy

Before starting, prepare a solid social media strategy for the following reasons:

Craft Engaging Content

Interact with customers effectively.

Boost Sales

Your plan should detail the platforms and tools to

achieve your communication and goals. Stick to it, avoid excessive posts, and center messages around your objectives.

Are there businesses that became successful using social media? Let's check the following success stories.

Case Study: GoPro

GoPro uses social media as a marketing strategy. It taps the platform to advocate for its catchphrase, "The world's most versatile camera." It uses the networks to get ahead of its competitors.

GoPro targets a diverse customer base through different social media platforms. By sharing customer-generated content, they showcase their product's value and quality. GoPro's unique social media approach focuses on advertising, product value, and customer communication. They gain trust by sharing product images and daily activities.

On Twitter, their #GoProMillionDollarChallenge hashtag campaign boosts engagement through user-generated videos and mentions.

GoPro annually hosts awards for user-submitted footage across various categories on their website. Winners receive awards. The company also promotes the winners' content through social marketing channels. This way,

GoPro boosts its sales and contributes to its popularity on social media channels.

Case Study: Moz

Moz is a search engine optimization and social monitoring service provider. It uses gaming mechanics to drive writer and member participation. Points earned from posts, comments, and likes separate experts from the crowd. This approach fosters active participation for better rankings and uses social proof to gain visitor trust.

Case Study: Mercedes-Benz

Mercedes-Benz's standout social media campaign from 2013 targeted a younger audience. It hired five top Instagram photographers to drive a new CLA model. The photographer with the most likes won the car.

The campaign resulted in 2 million new Instagram likes and 150 marketing-worthy photos. Also, it generated 87 million organic impressions.

Case Study: Disney

Disney captivates various demographics by creating targeted content. For instance, they have the *Star Wars* revival for older and younger generations. They engage fans through platforms like Instagram. At the same time, Disney targets younger *Frozen* fans through consumer goods and toys. These strategies, fueled by social media, have generated millions in revenue for Disney.

Case Study: Orabrush

Dr. Bob Wagstaff's innovative tongue brush began to gain traction when he tried YouTube. With just a $500 investment, his 2-minute video garnered 16 million views. Also, it generated $1.6 million in sales, leading to contracts with Walmart and CVS Pharmacies.

Key lessons include the following:

- addressing a relatable issue (bad breath)

- keeping videos brief

- embedding them on your home page

- capturing attention quickly

- offering a free incentive

Orabrush's website effectively incorporates user-generated video stories and press quotes. These campaigns highlight their successful YouTube channel. Additionally, they keep customers engaged by integrating Facebook into their site.

You now know how these companies became successful through social media. They use the platform to interact with customers and generate and share their reviews. If they were successful, there's no reason for you not to try it. Use social media with your review strategy to boost business success.

How I Made My Client's Customers Trust Incentivized Reviews for Their Business

I allow my consulting client to use incentivized reviews, which help their business. Here's how I designed a program to ensure their customers still trust my client's company.

First, my client only offers discount coupons as incentives. They refrain from giving away their products or services for free. Why? I want people to know that these incentivized reviewers used their money to buy my client's offerings.

Second, I tell my client to ask customers to write honest reviews whenever they give discounts. They don't impose that the reviewers report only positive features. My client won't be able to improve their business if they demand that their incentivized customers only share nice things about their products or services.

Third, I ask my client to tell incentivized reviewers to state in their reviews that they purchased the product at a discount. By being honest and transparent, I want the customers to see my client's business as trustworthy.

Fourth, my client allows constructive criticism. Thus, potential customers understand if a specific product or service suits their needs. This way, my client also reduces the number of negative reviews because their customers have prior knowledge before purchasing.

There's nothing wrong with offering incentives for reviews, but you should be transparent about it. Aside from boosting your online presence, use them to improve your business. However, remember that you should check the terms of service of third-party review platforms if they allow incentivized reviews.

Unfortunately, with the amount of customer reviews online, you can't read and assess each one. You need tech tools to help you.

Chapter 10:

Step 8—Use Review Tech Tools

It's not a faith in technology. It's faith in people. –Steve Jobs

Having the appropriate resources is essential to handle and use client feedback efficiently. A range of review technology tools can help you oversee and control customer evaluations. Using these instruments simplifies your evaluation procedures. Also, they transform client input into a potent mechanism for development and progress.

This step will discuss the various tools you can use in your business. You'll learn the features, benefits, and disadvantages of each. But what should you look for in a customer feedback management app?

Top Criteria in Choosing the Most Suitable Software for Customer Review Management

What factors do you consider when choosing the ideal customer review management platform? Here's a rundown of the assessment criteria:

- *User interface (UI)*: Search for user-friendly systems for businesses and customers.

- *Usability*: The best tools should be user-friendly and with an extensive set of features.

- *Integrations*: Be on the lookout for seamless connections with widely used business tools.

- *Value for money*: Find budget-friendly online solutions for businesses of all sizes.

Now you know the criteria, your next step is to learn the features to look for in an app.

Features to Look for in a Customer Feedback Management Platform

Here are some key features to look for in a top-notch business reputation management system:

- *Collecting reviews*: a simple method for customers to post their feedback online, making it easy to gather and showcase

- *Displaying reviews*: the option to show customer testimonials on the company website or other platforms

- *Tracking and monitoring*: the software identifying feedback across different channels

- *Unified management dashboard*: a centralized hub allowing admins to oversee all functions effortlessly

- *Handling customer feedback*: offering efficient solutions to address and manage customer responses

- *Instant notifications*: real-time updates on new reviews and other platform activities

- *Analysis and reporting*: comprehensive data on the source and content of reviews

I've lined up some customer review management software for you. Check their features and pros and cons. I hope you find the one you need.

Top Customer Review Management Applications

Jotform Enterprise

Jotform Enterprise is a user-friendly, cloud-powered form automation platform. It enables users to generate, customize, and share various online forms through different channels. At the same time, it gathers customer feedback.

Its analytical and reporting capabilities offer valuable data for survey teams. Such information helps produce leads, conduct market research, and register event attendees. It also oversees job applications and handles customer reviews.

This is best for large companies.

Features

- *w*ide selection of ready-made templates for many use cases

- customizable templates using the user-friendly form builder

- integration with popular business tools

- forms are also available on mobile phone

- other features like data analysis, reports, white labeling single sign-on (SSO), and others

Advantages

- *i*mproved back-end features

- excellent form creator

Disadvantages

- *p*oor customer service

- expensive

- forms not mobile-friendly

Birdeye

Birdeye is a customer experience platform designed to help you get more reviews automatically. Then, it turns feedback into a compelling advantage. The software sends customers to top review sites to share their feedback.

This is best for local businesses.

Features

- easily accessible online

- captures survey responses in real-time

- integration with Google API and other apps

Advantages

- responsive and helpful customer support

- effectively manages reviews

- free Demo

Disadvantages

- not user-friendly

ReviewTrackers

ReviewTrackers is a trusted and effective reputation and review management platform. It enhances customer acquisition and retention efforts. Key functionalities encompass review gathering, competitor analysis, media observation, and notifications.

This is best for competitive market analysis.

Features

- provides actionable insights for competitor comparisons

- reviews widgets, performance analytics, and review requests through texts

- collects reviews from many third-party platforms

- integration with popular business tools

Advantages

- outstanding customer support

- user-friendly

Disadvantages

- delay in extracting and updating reviews after replying

- the mobile app not refreshing

Grade.us

Grade.us is a cloud-based reputation management platform offering automation of review management.

Features include feedback collection, multichannel control, and gathering social proof.

This is best for agencies managing customers' reputations.

Features

- review reporting tools

- customized performance report and monitoring metrics

- integration with popular business tools

- free trial

Advantages

- outstanding customer support

- user-friendly and scalable

Disadvantages

- no deep-linking capability

Podium

Podium serves as a customer interaction platform dedicated to assisting local businesses. It helps in maintaining their digital presence. This user-friendly SaaS solution offers tools to improve customer satisfaction. Also, it supports local SEO.

A central aspect of the platform is generating online reviews. It motivates customers to share their thoughts on the products and services provided.

This is best for local businesses.

Features

- *i*ncludes payment processing, web chat, and SMS marketing

- customized review collection and personalized text conversations

- integration with popular business tools

- free trial

Advantages

- *u*ser-friendly

- can assign tasks to different employees

Disadvantages

- mobile app glitches

- tedious cancellation of subscription

Yotpo

Yotpo is a well-liked content marketing tool for ecommerce companies. It produces valuable feedback and recommendations. This platform makes gathering reviews a breeze through email and SMS channels.

This is best for local businesses.

Features

- detailed insights about customer sentiment and conversion rates

- integration with popular e-commerce platforms

- free trial

Advantages

- outstanding customer support

- user-friendly

Disadvantages

- expensive

Rize Reviews

Rize Reviews offers a handy reviews widget showing client testimonials. The platform gathers evaluations and ratings from online sources. You can customize your desired widget appearance and decide if you want to display the overall review score.

This is best for widgets that collect reviews.

Features

- accessible to users across several platforms and channels

- custom brand messaging and flexible targeting

- integration with standard business tools

- automatic review monitoring

- personalized email campaigns

- free demo

Advantages

- user-friendly

- outstanding customer support

Disadvantages

- no big issue

Trustpilot Business

Trustpilot serves as a valuable tool for managing customer experiences. It assists businesses in handling customer communication and issuing review requests.

Also, it helps in overseeing business listings, sharing testimonials, and monitoring responses.

This is best for real-time analysis of customer feedback.

Features

- rule configuration for sending review invites
- availability of newsletters, email signatures, and widgets
- real-time analysis of customer feedback
- integration with many business tools
- free plan available

Advantages

- outstanding platform for customer reviews

Disadvantages

- training needed for the customer support team

Get More Reviews

Get More Reviews is a user-friendly, cloud-supported review administration platform. It assists businesses in producing and handling online evaluations. Key features include the following:

- a negative review filter

- email organization

- automated social media sharing

This is best for companies that need an all-in-one solution.

Features

- real-time alerts for feedback management

- notification alert for negative reviews for a quick resolution

- integration with third-party social media applications

- free trial

Advantages

- user-friendly

- affordable

Disadvantages

- no refund or partial billing

- cancellation should be before the billing period

Merchant Centric

Merchant Centric handles responses from your website, call centers, surveys, and online evaluations. Feel free to incorporate your unique brand identity and tailor content for specific brands or locations.

This is best for companies that need reviews collection with a link.

Features

- immediate notification of negative feedback through alerts

- collate feedback from customers with a single link

- free trial

- integration with many widely used business platforms

Advantages

- excellent dashboard

- outstanding customer support

Disadvantages

- no self-service SEO

- need to go through the customer support team to request changes

Voice of the Customer Tools

Customer feedback solutions, such as voice of the customer (VoC) tools, have become essential for online businesses. They help in enhancing customer experience efforts. These tools facilitate seamless communication for users to share their experiences. They do so without disrupting their online journey. Furthermore, they're excellent for gathering real-time feedback.

Eager to kick off your customer voice initiative? Give one of these tools a go.

Mopinion

Mopinion is a comprehensive user feedback solution for all your online platforms. This customer-centric software instantly gathers and examines reviews from the following:

- websites

- mobile applications

- email campaign feedback

Mopinion boasts an effortless interface. Users can create, design, and tailor feedback forms to their preferences.

- conversational feedback

- sending of feedback forms to a specific group

- customizable charts and dashboard

- quick response to reviews through intelligent alerts

Advantages

- customizable survey forms

- scalable

Disadvantages

- poor customer support

Feedier

Feedier (IXM) provides the ultimate user-friendly experience management tool. It helps you pay close attention to the VoC to enhance your customer experience.

Features

- real-time collection of direct and indirect reviews

- gamified forms

- visual and intuitive dashboard

- data analysis using keywords, user stories, correlation matrix, NPS, and more

Advantages

- user-friendly

- outstanding customer support

Disadvantages

- confusing terminologies used in the app

- time-consuming to learn for some users

Feedbackify

Feedbackify provides a website feedback platform focused on the VoC. It allows companies to connect with their customers when they need it most. Also, it features a user-friendly, drag-and-drop system for organizing customer feedback categories. It also includes a comprehensive reporting dashboard.

Features

- drag-and-drop editor

- customizable review templates

- real-time viewing of reviews

Advantages

- data privacy

- integration with most business tools

- intuitive dashboard

Disadvantages

- user interface upgrade needed

InMoment

InMoment provides a versatile cloud-supported platform for enhancing customer experiences. Also, it features the following:

- services such as social reviews and advocacy

- employee engagement applications

- a VoC software

Features

- action planning

- active listening studio

- data exploration

- online reports

- real-time incidence management and alerts

- integration with popular e-commerce tools

Advantages

- outstanding customer support

- customizable reports

- user-friendly

Disadvantages

- steep learning curve for new users

Clarabridge

Clarabridge has been an all-inclusive customer experience and digital interaction platform. It provides a decade of top-notch speech and text analytics solutions. Also, it uses AI, machine learning, and intelligent algorithms.

Clarabridge helps you in uncovering valuable insights from massive amounts of data. Qualtrics acquired Clarabridge in 2021.

Features

- data analytics

- measures customer effort

- sentiment analysis

- feedback segmentation

- digital engagement

- centralized inbox

- service-level agreement monitoring

- routing capabilities

- integration with popular platforms

Advantages

- user-friendly

- outstanding customer support

Disadvantages

- fewer platform features

- perceived as rigid by some users

Verint Experience Management

Verint Experience Management is a management tool for customer experience. It enables you to track customer experience analytics through a streamlined process consistently. The Verint Experience Cloud provides an array of VoC functionalities.

Moreover, this software excels in delivering benchmarking and competitive data analysis.

Features

- can integrate with popular business solutions

- available in mobile versions

- case management offering solutions based on rule-based criteria

- team collaboration, root cause analysis, and ratings

- performance metrics, heat maps, benchmarking, and review collection

Advantages

- user-friendly

- offers various ways of extracting real-time feedback

- helpful competitor analysis and benchmarking

Disadvantages

- challenging navigation as it requires a mouse

- not intuitive

- slow

Wootric

Wootric, a part of the InMoment family, offers customer experience management software. It features single-question micro surveys. Usually, these surveys measure key performance indicators.

Once you gather the feedback, you'll see the reviews on the live dashboard for assessment. Wootric can be a different product for companies looking to boost their VoC program.

Features

- SMS and email marketing

- import and export of data

- review collection

- data analytics

- multichannel and multi-language platform

- NPS trends

Advantages

- user-friendly

- intuitive

- use of tags to categorize data

Disadvantages

- not possible to compare current and previous data

- mobile application not responsive

This list has provided valuable insights into choosing the right customer feedback tools. Like many other improvement plans, execute your customer review management program consistently.

You should constantly gather feedback across all appropriate digital channels. Assess reviews using your charts and dashboards to reconnect with your customers.

But not all customer feedback tools offer a scamless way to analyze and act upon your feedback within their software. Thus, you must choose carefully and ensure your application fits your needs.

Efficient management of customer reviews shouldn't be your only goal. You have a wealth of information in your hands. How do you use it to improve your business? Next, we'll discuss how to use these reviews for feedback and improvement.

Chapter 11:

Step 9—Use Customer Reviews as a Tool for Feedback and Improvement

Practice the philosophy of continuous improvement. Get a little bit better every single day. —Brian Tracy

Using testimonials to get feedback and promote progress lets you identify expansion opportunities. Also, you gain a crucial understanding of elevating the client journey.

You can boost customer contentment and devotion. You also profit by assessing and implementing the input received.

In this step, you can better understand how to use customer feedback for improvement. But first, let's talk about customer experience and its significance.

Customer Experience and Its Importance

What was your most recent encounter as a client? To address this inquiry, you may begin by recalling your previous interaction. Where did it occur? Who provided it? How will you describe your level of enjoyment?

If that encounter was exceptional, pleasant recollections filled your thoughts. It's easy to describe it without needing to recollect much.

But if your experience was awful, your brain will transport you to the emotional memories. You may feel anger, disappointment, and so on. It can lead you to criticize the company or establishment responsible for the negative experience.

This concept also applies to your clients. If you can offer them an outstanding customer experience, they will become your promoters at no extra cost! Indeed, you can excel in providing exceptional customer experience and boost your revenue by 4–8% (Bain & Company, 2015).

What Is Customer Experience?

A customer experience is the associated emotions and impressions a customer has from a buying experience.

The feelings can come from singular and ongoing encounters with a company's staff, systems, channels, or products.

There are two vital components to concentrate on in customer experience. The first is your clientele, and the second is your offering. Customers will appreciate your company and products or services if you meet their needs and ensure quality.

Why Is Customer Experience Essential to Your Business?

The significance of customer experience spans various aspects. Here's how it contributes to business expansion:

- aids in boosting revenue

- assists in cutting expenses

- facilitates the growth of earnings

- strengthens customer loyalty

- decreases customer attrition

Delivering an exceptional customer experience yields these benefits. Let's dive deeper into each of them.

Increases Revenue

Enhanced customer experiences directly contribute to increased sales. Walker's research revealed that by the end of 2020, customer experience would surpass product and price as a primary factor in brand differentiation (Walker, n.d.).

The study indicates that customer experience disrupts the traditional price–demand relationship. This disruption can decrease the demand with rising prices and vice versa. Customers with a positive experience are less inclined to change brands for future purchases.

Additionally, consumers often are willing to spend more for goods and services they are loyal to. It aids in guaranteeing that businesses maintain strong sales from returning customers.

Cuts Costs

Providing an exceptional experience for your clients aids in decreasing expenses. Which expenses? The costs of gaining more clients, keeping them from leaving, and promoting your brand.

You know that obtaining a new client can be 5–25 times costlier than keeping a current one, based on your sector (Gallo, 2014).

Contented customers will serve as your brand representatives. They can share their outstanding experiences with friends and acquaintances. Essentially, they can promote your brand indirectly.

But a poor customer experience increases costs. You need to reestablish the relationship to keep the displeased clients.

Increases Profits

Individuals are often willing to spend extra for an enhanced customer experience. It isn't just about a select group of wealthy individuals who splurge on anything they fancy.

A premium is likely to be paid by 86% of individuals for an exceptional customer experience (Stattin, 2023). Concentrating on customer experience can boost your profit margins and increase your earnings. Thus, adopt a customer-focused strategy for higher income and business growth. Provide an experience to your customers wherein they're eager to pay more.

Boosts Customer Loyalty

Do you know the common factor among many thriving businesses? A solid base of devoted customers. These loyal customers are your happiest and most content clients. Existing customers contribute to 65% of a company's revenue (McCain, 2023).

As mentioned earlier, satisfied customers become your promotional ambassadors. They continue to patronize your business and share positive feedback about them within their circles.

A popular trend these days is that the most dedicated customers create video reviews of the products and share them on YouTube. A viral video can attract more clients and support the product's lasting success. Research indicates that 75% of loyal customers suggest a brand to their friends and family (InMoment, n.d.).

An outstanding customer experience fosters increased customer loyalty. It leads to more committed customers referring your brand to their acquaintances. In the end, it can result in business improvement.

Reduces Customer Attrition

Would you consider leaving a brand that always offers an incredible customer experience? Of course not! Besides, when you provide an outstanding experience for your customers, you increase their lifetime value. They become less likely to switch to another brand.

Strive to offer exceptional customer service to retain customers. A survey reveals that 93% of customers are more likely to become loyal, returning clients (Redbord, 2022).

After all, everyone desires happiness. If a customer experience can bring them joy, they'd want to relive that experience. Generally, you measure customer experience from client feedback. Thus, we've been discussing customer reviews in this book.

We discussed gathering and sharing them in previous sections, but how do they help improve your business?

Using Customer Feedback to Improve Your Business

Gaining knowledge from your clients' perspectives is essential for market understanding. Discover ways to use customer input directly and indirectly to implement improvements. If you do so, you're bound for a successful expansion.

Improve Online Customer Experience

User experience (UX) goes beyond website design. It encompasses the way all elements of your site work together. It's common for business owners and web designers to overlook a bug or hiccup, despite thorough testing.

Nonetheless, users will likely encounter issues your testing team may need to catch up on. Moreover, something a tech-savvy tester might not view as a problem could cause difficulties for visitors to your website.

Users who encounter a bug or glitch need a quick method to contact your support team. Use the following means to simplify how customers report issues:

Implement Automatic Error Notifications

First, these notifications are a popular strategy for gathering UX feedback. If you've ever been scrolling through an app and experienced a crash, you probably received a message about the error. Generally, this alert allows sending your data to the team for assessment.

Incorporate a Contact Form

Second, an efficient means of asking your audience for feedback is to have an easy-to-use online contact form on your website.

Distribute Follow-Up Emails

Third, periodically send emails to your subscribers. You can also email new customers requesting feedback about their experiences. Inquire what they would alter about their experience if given a chance. This information is valuable for growing your business and making your clients happy.

Create Social Influence

Social proof is that individuals are more inclined to buy when they observe others buying and using items from the same company. There are many methods to develop social proof through customer input, such as the following:

Develop Testimonial Sections

First, testimonial sections show prospective clients why your company deserves their attention. Use the feedback acquired through contact forms to create testimonial sections for your site.

Analyze Your Social Media Channels

Second, customers offer valuable insight when they communicate with you. It establishes social proof or improves your operations. Knowing how your target clients perceive your brand and offerings is vital to connecting with them.

Address Online Evaluations

Third, online assessments are public discussions like social media interactions and comments. You should reply to online evaluations, both positive and negative, to show how you handle different kinds of feedback.

Regardless of the comments left by your clientele, engage with as many individuals as possible. Remember to consider their viewpoints. Those who provide feedback have either had a fantastic customer experience or wish to convey how you can enhance your services.

Develop Your Product Line

As your enterprise expands, plan on adding more goods or services. Focus on customers' opinions before developing a new product or incorporating one into your offerings. Take, for instance, an online pet store receiving several inquiries about when they will include dog and cat treats.

Such feedback is valuable and indicative of customer satisfaction. But customers want more offerings. In this case, you would explore integrating top-notch pet treats into your growing product catalog.

Regardless of your sector or niche, feedback can drive growth. You can improve conversion rates, sales, and customer retention by listening to your customers. Then, you should incorporate the sought-after products or features.

Raise the Level of Customer Service

Here are a few suggestions for leveraging client input to enhance the assistance you provide to customers in the future:

Use Feedback From Contact Forms to Educate Your Support Staff

First, inform your team about the usual concerns customers raise when submitting contact forms. If a large part of these forms has similar questions or grievances, it means many customers face the same issue.

Assist your team in developing a quick, effective solution for this issue, or share the answer in your guidelines, FAQs, or self-help section.

Actively Request Feedback After a Purchase

Second, promptly ask for input following a sale to tackle issues directly. You should do so before the client becomes annoyed, leaves a negative review, or chooses not to continue doing business with you.

Improve your Chatbot Using Customer Insights

Third, if you use a chatbot, feedback can aid in programming and fine-tuning your bot to address common inquiries or worries. The finest live chat software provides various customization choices to meet your needs.

Study New Markets

When considering broadening your range of products or launching new sites, it's a great idea to seek input from your customers. It will help you gauge the level of interest in a new offering or the potential success of your business in a specific region.

Take Trader Joe's grocery store as an example; they have an online form allowing customers to suggest a location for a new store. If several requests come in for a specific area, they can investigate further to determine if they should establish a new store there.

Make Your Customers Happy

Asking clients for input shows you respect their opinions. Also, it lets them know that you put their satisfaction first. Strengthen ˏ this bond by communicating the improvements made due to their suggestions.

Complete the feedback cycle, and thank the customers for their involvement to boost your connection with them. In turn, you generate higher sales, favorable evaluations, and referrals.

How I Designed the Procedure for My Client to Collect Customer Feedback

As my consulting client grew their business, they realized tracking all customer feedback and requests was challenging. They wanted to follow several channels where their customers could discuss their company.

So I researched and tried various apps with my client's tech team. Currently, they use Productboard and integrate it with Slack. Check its features and capabilities to see if it fits your requirements.

You may also research other apps. The primary thing here is that you should use technology to collect these reviews. Doing so lets you collect customer feedback and use the insights for improvement.

Using customer reviews to improve your business is necessary to generate more income and boost profits. With what you learned from this step, you now know how to use them to make your company successful.

Unfortunately, improving your business isn't a one-time deal. You should strive for continuous improvement. Therefore, engaging your customers should also be part of your daily procedures. Spend time responding to reviews to create a positive impact.

Chapter 12:

Step 10—Respond to Reviews and Create a Positive Impact

Thank your customer for complaining and mean it. Most will never bother to complain. They'll just walk away. –Marilyn Suttle

Engaging with feedback helps you improve your online reputation and visibility. Responding to evaluations and using SEO-driven responses can boost search engine rankings. Addressing negative feedback and resolving customer issues can turn a negative into a positive.

Encouraging satisfied customers to update their reviews reflects the commitment to customer contentment. Also, it helps attract new clients and positive word-of-mouth recommendations.

We'll discuss how you can respond to different reviews next.

Responding to All Reviews: Timely, SEO-Rich Comments

Customer reviews provide valuable insights, and responding to them builds client trust. Your visible business response can prompt the reviewer to receive a notification. It allows them to read your message and update their review.

Why You Should Reply to Reviews

Negative reviews on Google Business reviews can impact customer decisions. To improve your online reputation, respond to reviews as a cost-free strategy. Let's explore the six reasons for addressing these reviews.

Boosts Local SEO and Google Rankings

First, online review responses enhance local SEO, raising the likelihood of ranking in Google Maps' top three local results. These signals account for 15.44% of Google's Local Pack rankings, with timely responses boosting your position (Barloso, 2020).

Google affirms that addressing reviews shows customer gratitude and increases visibility. It also attracts potential clients.

Improves Customer Trust

Second, if you respond to reviews, your customer will feel valued. Your response is proof you provide exceptional service for your clients.

Most consumers (53.3%) expect a response within seven days. They perceive businesses that do so as 1.7 times more trustworthy (ReviewTrackers, 2022b). Responses by companies to reviews are read by 88% of consumers. As such, timely replies benefit the reviewer and other potential customers (Paget, 2023).

Strive to reply immediately to make your customers see your business as a trustworthy company. People will patronize you if you prove you're worthy of their trust.

Possibly Reverses Negative Reviews

Third, responding to feedback like Google reviews can lead to negative reviews becoming positive. Sometimes, the customer may even delete it. A Harris study revealed that 33% of customers changed their negative feedback to positive ones. Also, 34% deleted them after receiving a response (Collier, 2011).

Negative reviews are sometimes good for business and can offer a chance to convert unhappy customers into satisfied ones.

Limits Negative Feedback

Fourth, responding to reviews can reduce negative feedback. But ignoring negative feedback can harm your company. You can see it with Nestlé's environmental practices debacle (McCarthy, 2010). Acknowledging and addressing negative reviews shows attentiveness.

Thus, customers will think twice about leaving a negative review for a minor issue. Others will see them as chronic complainers. Constant complainers never influence other people not to patronize a business.

Raises Review Ratings

Fifth, responding to online reviews boosts Google ratings and encourages more feedback. A Tripadvisor study in 2018 found that review responses increased review quantity by 12% and ratings by 0.12 stars (Proserpio & Zervas, 2018). It demonstrates the positive impact of engaging with reviewers.

Receives Real-Time Feedback

Sixth, swift responses to Google reviews can foster real-time interactions. They also yield vital feedback and business insights. Rapid replies to online reviews boost local SEO and Google rankings.

Address all reviews by demonstrating gratitude and

consideration. This practice helps establish a reliable, customer-focused brand image. You must learn how to respond to reviews and determine the appropriate response type.

Which Response Is Suitable for a Customer Review?

Customer reviews are critical for a business's stature and success in today's digital world. As an entrepreneur, you must understand the proper response for each feedback. Create perfect replies to boost your online presence and build strong client relationships. Master the ideal reaction for increased customer loyalty and contentment.

But there's no one-size-fits-all response when it comes to customer reviews. Before writing your reply, you must learn the different reactions to know which suits a specific situation. I list eight kinds.

No Response

First, the no-response type can be detrimental to your business. If you ignore the reviews, expect any or all of the following can happen:

- unacknowledged feedback

- unthanked customers

- unaddressed rude language or misinformation

Not replying can harm the company's image and show indifference toward customers.

Negative Reply to a Negative Feedback

Second, the negative-for-negative response is a reply you must always avoid. Negative reviews offer crucial insights for business improvement. But if you react angrily to them, you'll appear petty. More importantly, fighting fire with fire can lead to a public customer service disaster.

Generic Response

Third, a generic reply is a response you should avoid. Saying "thank you" to positive reviews and giving a generic answer to unsatisfied customers are valid. But customers and potential clients may doubt your company's sincerity in addressing complaints.

Grammatically Incorrect Response

Fourth, grammatically incorrect replies reflect poorly on your company's professionalism. Grammar, spelling, and prose errors can undermine great content. If your business neglects communication details, will you care about service quality?

Robotic Reply

Fifth, template-based or machine-written responses can upset unhappy customers seeking genuine human interaction. Such impersonal interactions may deter future customers. Potential customers may perceive your in-person service as cold.

Overzealous Response

Sixth, a passionate reply can overwhelm customers. Even if you're passionate about your clients, avoid overdoing your responses. Treat customers respectfully and avoid lengthy all caps paragraphs. Also, don't pepper your reply with excessive thank-yous, emojis, and exclamation points.

Missed-SEO-Opportunity Reply

Seventh, the missed-SEO-opportunity response fulfills basic requirements. But it needs SEO keywords such as business name, products, and services. While adequate for customer service, it doesn't contribute to SEO optimization.

Expertly Written Response

Eighth, professional, SEO-optimized, expert-written responses are the ideal replies to thank customers. They also enhance local search rankings and increase engagement and conversions.

Knowing the types of responses is only meaningful if you know how to use them to reply to positive reviews.

How to Respond to Positive Reviews

Respond to all reviews, not only negative ones, to avoid pushing unfavorable content to the top of your page. Engage with satisfied customers through positive responses. Remember to maintain the conversation after the sale to increase the likelihood of repeat business.

Follow these tips to reply to positive customer reviews:

Include Keywords

Responding to a positive review lets you include pertinent keywords in your Google Business Profile. Typically, local business keywords include the company name, location, products, and services.

Add Personal Touch

Incorporating the reviewer's name in your reply adds a warm, personal touch. However, as a rule of thumb, you can only share the name if the review is public.

Repeat the Product in the Response

Should the client refer to the brand or type they bought, kindly incorporate it in your feedback reply. If you're uncertain about the product the client acquired, it's best to avoid assumptions!

Include Other Products

Another method to use your positive review response is suggesting other items the client might want to get later. Incorporating too many keywords can be tempting. Ensure that the supplementary product you endorse benefits the person who wrote the review.

Mention Your Corporate Values

Identify fundamental company principles, such as a seamless purchasing experience. Use review responses to showcase these values to potential clients browsing your feedback.

Replying to a positive customer review should be a

breeze, but do you know how to respond to negative feedback?

How to Reply to Negative Feedback

Positive reviews boost a brand, while negative ones can damage its reputation. But negative reviews offer chances for growth and enhancement. You can lessen the negative impact by addressing dissatisfied customers professionally and tactfully. It can also showcase your dedication to excellent customer service.

So let's dive into managing criticism with grace and effectiveness!

Be Professional

Avoid seeming defensive, emotional, or sarcastic. Don't include personal opinions on sensitive topics. Keep review responses professional, neutral, and friendly.

Avoid Publicly Accusing the Reviewer of Fraud

Fake reviews happen, but handling them like other negative feedback is crucial. Report suspicious reviews through proper channels. You can request Google to remove negative reviews if they violate Google's review policy.

Apologize for the Reviewer's Frustrations

Apologize when necessary. Focus on the customer's distress, and address the issue through direct communication. Show empathy without admitting fault, acknowledging several perspectives for future readers.

Offer a Plan

In situations where it's appropriate, inform the customer that you intend to act promptly. It readies the customer for your upcoming call. Also, it demonstrates your eagerness to take the initiative with prospective clients.

Avoid Speculation

When a client shows frustration without stating the reason, avoid assumptions. Acknowledge their unhappiness, and kindly ask for more details about their issue during the phone call.

You already know the best practices for dealing with negative feedback. But how do you handle neutral ones?

How to Reply to Neutral Reviews

Impartial assessments often combine praise and constructive feedback, necessitating tailored review response strategies. Neutral evaluations are usually brief and need more details. Clients may want to refrain from explaining their experiences.

What should be a suitable response to neutral feedback? I list the following best practices:

Be Grateful

In initiating your balanced review reply, thank the customer for their effort in composing their feedback.

Emphasize the Positive

In your reply, emphasize good points in a 3-star review, like, "Glad our product met your expectations." Acknowledge positive aspects even in negative feedback.

Deal With the Negative

If you get an impartial review with unfavorable remarks, recognize the client's problems. It's also a good idea to offer a brief apology and share a short clarification about the situation.

Privately Take the Conversation Offline

Request further customer information for a detailed investigation. Also, it prevents public exposure to harmful experiences and effectively manages customer experience.

Sometimes, you can turn hostile or neutral feedback into a positive one. How do you do it?

How to Encourage Customers to Update Their Reviews

Address negative feedback by connecting with dissatisfied customers. Apologize and understand their issues, showing empathy and ensuring they feel heard. Try to correct the situation, prevent a recurrence, and kindly request a review revision or removal.

Offer a complimentary *redo* to make the situation right. Then, talk to your customer about the *redo* experience. They may provide feedback if the business has met or exceeded their expectations. Keep a friendly, nonaggressive tone and avoid enticing or intimidating customers.

You should respond to all reviews because it's part of reputation management. If you want your company to flourish, learn to protect your brand.

Reputation Management: Responding to Reviews and Addressing Concerns

Reputation management occurs on different online platforms, involving client sales rep interactions. Managing these discussions can be daunting due to limited control and many channels. But several tools and strategies exist to protect your brand and reputation.

Before we delve deeper, let's first define reputation management.

What Is Reputation Management?

Managing your business reputation involves maintaining a company's image. It's an essential facet of running a business due to online discussions. Strategies include addressing or suppressing online messages, SEO, social media, and public relations.

A positive reputation fosters customer loyalty, revenue growth, and expansion. Negative reputations can damage sales and retention. But they can offer insights for improving business operations to serve customers better.

The key to a strong reputation is simple: Respond to all feedback. Your reputation is valuable; one bad review can drive away 30 potential clients. You surely don't want to turn off new customers, do you? So make it a habit to respond to client feedback.

You should develop an effective reputation management strategy. Ensure your team knows the correct ways and timings for handling reviews.

How to Craft a Reputation Management Strategy

A robust reputation management strategy is vital for success, regardless of business size or industry. Your stature is your most treasured asset, and maintaining and improving it is crucial.

This section will discuss creating an effective strategy to protect your image. It will also boost your online presence for growth.

Assign Obligations and Duties

Regardless of whether you take care of review responses at the location level, delegate the task to a manager. You can assign it to your corporate team or entrust it to an agency. Always pay attention to the reviews.

Hold Meetings With Your Team

Your clients shared their experiences with your company. What should you do? Acknowledge staff who contributed to outstanding experiences. If you encounter negative feedback, learn from it and improve your services.

Also, use customer feedback data to address concerns. Remember to involve your team in understanding client opinions by discussing trending topics.

Openly Communicate With Clarity and Compassion

Publicly addressing reviews shows potential clients you value their experience and feedback. Own any mistakes, avoid blame, and offer solutions when appropriate. It can turn unsure customers into loyal supporters.

Be Consistent With Your Voice

Collaborate with your team to develop a tone and reply approach aligning with your brand, image, and location. The main goal is to provide a compassionate, personal, and human touch in your responses.

Being brief is fine, but avoid sounding cold and impersonal when replying to a review. Steer clear of short answers such as, "Thanks for your review."

How I Helped My Consulting Client Respond to a 1-Star Review

One irate customer posted an angry 1-star review on Google. Although it may seem justified to fight fire with fire, I recommended my consulting client to talk to their staff to ask their side. After knowing what happened, they immediately replied to the Google review.

First, they thanked their customer for their consideration. Then, they apologized for their customer's feelings of frustration. I asked my client to take the conversation out of the review platform. They asked their customer if they could call them to solve the issue.

Fortunately, they agreed. Since they already vented out their anger, the communication offline was amicable. They resolved the problem by offering a *redo* and offering a discount voucher for the customer's next visit. The customer was happy about the resolution of their case.

This customer updated their Google review and said they resolved the issue. They even thanked my client for fixing the problem immediately.

You learned why and how to respond to customer reviews in this step. Also, you now know what reputation management is and how to create a strategy.

We finished discussing the 10 core steps of *The Glowing Reviews Profit System*. If you follow them, you'll discover a glowing business soon. However, as your business grows and glows, you should ensure you shine with your company. The following section can help you invest in your health.

Chapter 13:

Glow With Your Business—Invest in Your Health to Boost Your Business

Never get so busy making a living that you forget to make a life.
–Dolly Parton

Taking care of yourself is essential if you want your business to thrive in the long run. That means making healthy choices and finding a good work–life balance. You can be more creative and productive when you feel good about yourself.

This section will discuss the significance of your health in making your business succeed. But you may wonder about the connection of wellness to business success. Let's dive in to get to know the answer.

The Connection Between Business Success and Wellness

Taking care of your well-being is crucial for your business's success. Focusing on your health will give you more energy and help you make better decisions for your entrepreneurial journey.

Neglecting your well-being as an entrepreneur can harm your business's success. That's why focusing on your health is crucial, as it can help you earn more money.

What if You Don't Focus on Your Physical and Mental Well-Being?

Being an entrepreneur can take a toll on both your body and mind. The constant demands of making difficult decisions can affect your well-being. Also, you become anxious about not getting immediate results from your invested money. It's common for entrepreneurs to lose sight of what truly matters and stretch themselves thin to find balance.

But dedicating all your time and effort to your business can negatively affect other aspects of your life. Give time for relaxation too. Putting all your focus on work can also result in stress and strain, harming your relationships and overall well-being.

Your poor business choices and financial setbacks can stress and strain relationships. To prevent these problems and find success as an entrepreneur, focus on your well-being. But extending this care to your employees' well-being is also essential.

Why You Should Prioritize Your Employees' Well-Being

Understanding the significance of employee well-being is vital for businesses. Prioritizing employee well-being can have positive effects on employee retention and recruitment.

The retention rate significantly impacts recruitment efforts. It even has a more significant effect than offering competitive salaries and benefits. Promoting positive mental health and reducing stress can create a healthier and more active workforce. It can result in improved focus on work.

Workplace absenteeism can significantly impact productivity levels. To address this issue, implement cost-effective initiatives. You can offer free fruit days or discounted gym memberships.

If you engage your employees, you can expect a boost in profits and productivity. Also, it reduces the likelihood of absenteeism compared to employees who need to be fully involved.

Embracing Health and Wellness as a Business Owner

You may have focused on your company before your well-being. Then, you recently discovered that concentrating on your overall health is also essential. A survey found that 58% of entrepreneurs face mental health challenges. They will likely suffer from anxiety, depression, and stress (Monae, 2022).

Moreover, 55% of respondents mentioned that running a business has harmed their mental well-being, and 71% reported higher-than-average stress levels in their daily work life (Monae, 2022). Don't become part of the statistics. Prioritize your overall health too.

While striving for success is natural, let's remember to focus on our health and happiness along the way.

Why You Must Focus on Your Health and Happiness Simultaneously With Your Business

If you want to avoid failure and not give up on your entrepreneurial path, it's crucial to remember these five facts and tips:

You Are Your Company's Biggest Asset

Focus on your overall well-being. While your resources may seem like your business's most crucial aspects, you must pay attention to your well-being. Mental health problems, exhaustion, and burnout can significantly diminish business value. So ensure you also focus on your well-being.

You Boost Your Motivation When You're Healthy

If you find yourself pressed for time to hit the gym, consider taking a leisurely walk as an easy exercise option. Pop in some earbuds, blast your favorite tunes, and experience the mood-boosting benefits of endorphins. Music can help clear your mind and uplift your spirits.

Aim to fit in at least three weekly workout sessions to stay active. It's also a good idea to swap out sugary sodas for water and make healthier food choices to maintain a balanced diet. And remember, sleep is also vital. It can enhance your productivity, energy levels, and focus.

Have a Support Group

Don't let negative people bring you down! Instead, focus on surrounding yourself with those who bring happiness and peace into your life, like your family and friends. If meeting in person isn't an option, why don't you try using Zoom meetings to connect?

You should build relationships with other entrepreneurs because they understand your situation. And if you don't have entrepreneur friends yet, consider joining or starting a group. It's an excellent way to support and connect on your entrepreneurial journeys.

Focus on Your Mental Health

If you feel something is amiss within yourself, don't disregard it. Reach out for help.

Take Time to Recharge

It's essential to relax, refresh, and recharge to avoid stress. As you know, stress can negatively impact our positive qualities and relationships. Discover activities that help you unwind and rejuvenate, such as reading, writing, or a soothing bath.

Make it a point to take short breaks from technology, and consider adding a 30-minute nap or a staycation to your routine. Remember, your mind and body should always be your first concern.

Opportunities for Improved Health and Wellness Through Business Growth

When starting a business, many people focus solely on its success without considering their well-being. But neglecting self-care can be as harmful as ignoring financial numbers or not finishing projects.

Even in a busy business, it is crucial to take care of oneself. Surprisingly, self-care should be a significant goal for any business. Unhealthy habits can harm productivity.

Why You Should Have a Good Mental State

Sustaining a positive mindset is critical for business owners. It can cultivate a robust leadership culture that enhances motivation, inspiration, and productivity. Thus, your business gains higher profitability and employee participation. It can reap the rewards of success by focusing on your physical and mental health.

Your mental well-being plays a crucial part in your business success. It empowers you and your employees to think outside the box and assess products and services thoughtfully. Encouraging employees to do the same is equally important.

Embracing digital innovation enables you to concentrate on essential tasks. Thus, it helps improve your mental health. It alleviates concerns about finances and creates space for growth strategies. Additionally, time-saving tools can boost productivity and precision and reduce stress caused by competition.

The Stress Caused by Competition

Competition is stressful for business owners. It's tough to operate in a competitive market, and it can be pretty draining. Thus, you need substantial financial resources to thrive, especially in economic crises. You should make intelligent strategic choices to run your company smoothly.

You can suffer significant losses due to financial mistakes and unexpected events. These losses may include unpaid invoices to suppliers. Also, such incidents can harm a company's reputation, requiring efforts to rebuild consumer trust.

To prevent these problems, focus on financial awareness. You can also use innovative, time-saving practical tools and software for gathering and organizing information.

Focus on What's Significant

Did you know that companies and employees can waste up to four days every month on tedious tasks like invoicing and data entry? It causes unnecessary stress and hampers employee engagement and overall business strategy.

To overcome this challenge, focus on efficiency. And guess what? Automation and digitization can be your best friends in achieving this goal!

Automation and digitization can help you delegate repetitive tasks to machines or algorithms. They also allow employees to spend valuable time on more meaningful, human-centric functions. Also, outsourcing tasks like data entry and filing to digital tools improves accuracy and security.

So if you want to create a more efficient and stress-free work environment, embracing automation and digitization is the way to go. It's time to free up your employees' time and let them focus on what truly matters—driving your business forward!

Automation is a great tool helping you maintain financial stability. It allows for cash flow management and growth and expansion planning. Not only does automation save time, but it also contributes to a healthy work–life balance for both business owners and employees.

By setting aside dedicated time for work and personal matters, you can focus on your products and services with peace of mind. This strategic approach reduces repetitive tasks. It gives you more time to build a strong company culture and drive growth.

How My Client Neglected Themselves but Bounced Back in Time

When my consulting client started their business 10 years ago, they worked hours and hours to keep it afloat. They thought they'd be successful sooner or later if they spent more time in operations.

Starting a business was very stressful. My client discovered that the harder they tried, the more stressed they became. Disappointment and frustration set in. They knew they had to snap out of whatever they were doing.

I told my client to ensure they have a healthy body and mind. They should go for an annual checkup of their physical and mental health. Moreover, I suggested a business and health coach to achieve optimal balance.

Fast forward to today, my client's business is thriving. They now maintain a healthy weight with nourishing food choices and exercise. They discovered that if they cared for their physical and mental health, their mind and body would be in tip-top shape to deal with business problems.

Thus, my last advice is to pay attention to yourself as you run your business. Ensure you're healthy to make solid decisions. I know it's a cliché, but health is wealth.

Conclusion

The Glowing Reviews Profit System allows you to generate more income and grow your business by focusing on customer feedback. Remember I discussed the R.E.V.I.E.W. method in the first part of my book. Let's recall them.

The R.E.V.I.E.W. Method

- *Research*: You should know your customers and their needs.

- *Engage*: You must communicate with your clients and offer exceptional service.

- *Value*: As a business owner, you can provide incentives for customers who leave honest feedback and reviews using company-owned platforms or on the reviewer's personal social media platform.

- *Improve*: You can only be successful if you continuously refine your products and services based on customer feedback.

- *Engage*: Make it a point to reply to positive and negative reviews. But always remember to be professional.

- *Win*: If you can satisfy your customers, they can become brand advocates.

This framework is the basis for the 10 core steps you learned. Let me reiterate them.

Step 1: Craft a 5-Star Customer Experience

Initially, you're enthusiastic about starting a business. But you soon realize running a company is always challenging. You must always deal with unsatisfied customers.

As an entrepreneur, you must realize that you must face challenging daily issues. You must be perceptive to discover how to make your clients brim with happiness.

Based on the research part of the R.E.V.I.E.W. method, your first step is to ask your clients about their needs and demands. Also, you can ask employees how your business can improve customer experience. Lastly, you can check what your competitors do to ensure customer satisfaction.

Once you determine the customer's demands, you can devise ways to continuously meet their expectations.

How can you ensure top-notch customer service? Here are some ways:

- Be responsive to customer requests and inquiries.

- Offer prompt and efficient service.

- Your frontline staff must be competent and courteous.

- Your business should be consistent in meeting customer expectations in all channels.

If you meet and exceed client expectations, you'll have loyal customers who can also be your brand advocates for free.

Step 2: Inquire How a Client Found You

As a small business owner, you should connect with your clients and understand how they discovered your business. Why? It helps you determine the areas and effective marketing channels where you can improve. For instance, if most customers find you on Facebook, you can direct your marketing efforts to this social media platform. This way, you don't waste resources on channels providing no value.

How will you ask your buyers? Here's a list of methods:

- Conduct surveys.

- Ask clients directly.

- Use search engines.

- Use Google Analytics.

- Observe your customers.

- Track your email list.

After knowing how your customers discovered your business, you can now analyze and make the necessary changes.

This second step also belongs to the research part of our R.E.V.I.E.W. method. It's crucial because you can direct your budget to marketing initiatives that bring out the best return for your money. Improve your marketing efforts to increase your customers and revenue.

Step 3: Assess Customer Satisfaction

Customer satisfaction is crucial for any business. It helps you understand where to improve, retain your valued customers, and boost your revenue. Moreover, it's also part of the research in our R.E.V.I.E.W. method. You can use surveys and metrics to understand the buyers' requirements.

Use the following to measure client satisfaction:

- customer satisfaction score

- customer churn rate

- customer lifetime value

- customer effort score

- Net Promoter Score

- customer health score

After understanding customer satisfaction, you can make necessary improvements and expand your business. Assessing customer satisfaction can drive business growth, reinforce retention, and boost customer loyalty.

Step 4: Engage Where Clients Are and Rake in Reviews

With your limited resources, you should use the internet to attract more customers and revenues. How? Turn to the first "E" (*Engage*) in our R.E.V.I.E.W. method.

Your business must interact actively with your clients. Give them different ways to communicate with you and share their feedback. For instance, most people are on Facebook. So why don't you create a Facebook business Page? You can also use Google and YouTube. If your goal is to generate positive online reviews, identify the appropriate platforms for your company.

Additionally, you can encourage your employees to advocate for reviews. It's an effective strategy to empower them to request feedback and share review links with clients.

You can create a steady flow of positive feedback by engaging with clients in a friendly manner and making it convenient for them to leave reviews. It can ultimately attract new customers and enhance your online reputation.

Step 5: Ask for Reviews

You must ask your customers for reviews to establish a solid online reputation and attract a more extensive customer base. Asking for reviews is which part of our R.E.V.I.E.W. method? Yes! It's still within the scope of our first "E" (*Engage*).

Some ways to request reviews include the following:

- asking in person

- email

- social media

- receipts and invoices

- third-party review platforms

- company website

Remember to follow these best practices when soliciting reviews:

- Be polite.

- Simplify the customer review process.

- Professionally handle negative reviews.

Find a suitable time to request feedback, and experience the rewards of your action. By doing so, you increase revenue, foster customer trust and loyalty, and enhance your online reputation.

Step 6: Share Customer Experiences on Your Social Media Accounts

Sharing positive customer experiences on social media can significantly impact business growth. It can establish trust with potential buyers and increase your online visibility. Also, you promote a strong sense of association around your brand. Do you recognize this step is part of our R.E.V.I.E.W. method's first "E" (*Engage*)?

Tap the power of social media to share customer experiences through the following:

- interviews
- video testimonials
- social media ads
- Stories and feed posts
- customer journey feature
- GIFs

To share customer reviews, opt for a short message. Use visuals and remember to thank the reviewer. Share the feedback on social media. Lastly, maintain a content calendar to optimize cross-promotion.

You must show customer testimonials to demonstrate how you provide value to clients. Actively immerse yourself with your clients on social networks. Remember to use their tools and features to share customer feedback effortlessly. Also, include this strategy in your social media marketing plan to generate and keep clients.

Step 7: Encourage Customers to Leave Reviews

Most satisfied customers don't write positive reviews. It's always the unsatisfied ones who are motivated to leave negative feedback. Thus, encourage happy clients to leave reviews. But how? We turn to the "V" (*Value*) in our R.E.V.I.E.W. method.

You should incentivize reviews and share positive experiences to boost review volume. Offering the following customer incentives can encourage feedback:

- free product

- early access to a product before the launch

- brand or store discounts

- brand or store loyalty points

Remember to inform your customers about the incentives. Also, for transparency, mark the incentivized review to inform the other clients. Once you have the feedback, analyze them to make the necessary adjustments to your business.

If you listen to feedback and make the necessary improvements, you also create better customer experiences. In the long run, you increase positive reviews and promote business growth.

Step 8: Use Review Tech Tools

The right tools are essential for effectively managing and using customer reviews. Luckily, many review tech tools can help you with your goals. These tools can track and handle customer reviews, engage with feedback, and enhance your online reputation.

You can simplify your review management process. Transform customer feedback into a valuable resource for growth and progress. Moreover, this step helps you improve how you manage your reviews. It's part of the "I" (*Improve*) of our R.E.V.I.E.W. method.

Step 9: Use Customer Reviews as a Tool for Improvement and Feedback

Customer reviews are a tool for feedback and improvement. They assist you in identifying growth areas. Also, you gain valuable insights to promote the customer experience. Carefully analyze the issues and create an action plan to boost revenue, loyalty, and customer satisfaction. This step falls under the "I" (*Improve*) of our R.E.V.I.E.W. method.

Step 10: Respond to Reviews and Create an Outstanding Impact

Your response to client feedback can boost your brand's visibility and your business's online reputation. Focus on replying to customer input for the following reasons:

- boosts local SEO and Google rankings

- improves customer trust

- reverses negative feedback

- reduces negative reviews

- increases review ratings

- receives real-time feedback

Learn to reply correctly to each form of feedback. When responding to positive feedback, remember to use the appropriate keywords. Mention your company's corporate values and products. Include a related item or service that the reviewer may like. Keep things personal by mentioning the name of the customer in your reply.

You should maintain your composure and professionalism if you get negative reviews. Apologize for the frustration the reviewer feels. Also, avoid speculations and publicly accusing the customer of giving fraudulent feedback. Always offer a plan to resolve the client's complaints.

For neutral feedback, always remember to thank the reviewer. Emphasize the good points, and deal with the negative ones. You can offer to take the discussion offline to resolve the issues faster.

This step falls under our second "E" (*Engage*) in our R.E.V.I.E.W. platform. It reminds you to interact with and acknowledge reviews actively. This way, you can demonstrate your commitment to client satisfaction.

Also, you create a favorable impact attracting new customers. More satisfied clients can recommend you to others through word-of-mouth referrals.

Glow With Your Business: Invest in Your Health to Boost Your Business

As a business owner, it's essential to make your health and well-being a top priority if you want to achieve lasting success. Healthy habits and balancing work and personal life can boost your energy. They can also increase your productivity and harness your creativity.

Also, as your business grows, you open doors to better health and wellness. How? You can plan team building, stress management initiatives, and flexible work arrangements. After all, a happy and healthy owner can better steer their business toward success.

By following the strategies in the R.E.V.I.E.W. blueprint, you can create a thriving enterprise and make a name for yourself in your industry. And once your business thrives, you can complete the "W" (*Win*) in our R.E.V.I.E.W. method. You no longer have to spend a sizable amount on marketing because you have loyal clients as your brand advocates.

Now that you know the 10 core steps to *The Glowing Reviews Profit System*, why don't you implement them today? Business success is now within reach.

To prove I practice what I preach, please leave a review if you enjoyed this book. Help me inspire more entrepreneurs to follow the R.E.V.I.E.W. blueprint. Also, I read all feedback with immense gratitude.

References

A-Z Quotes. (n.d.-a). *Top 25 blueprints quotes.* https://www.azquotes.com/quotes/topics/blueprints.html

A-Z Quotes. (n.d.-b). *Top 25 continuous improvement quotes (of 67).* https://www.azquotes.com/quotes/topics/continuous-improvement.html

A-Z Quotes. (n.d.-c). *"Wonder what customers really want? Ask. Don't tell." -Lisa Stone.* https://www.azquotes.com/quote/1353697

Adewolu, M. (2015, November 10). *5 reasons YouTube is the best place to obtain customer feedback.* Social Media Today. https://www.socialmediatoday.com/marketing/5-reasons-youtube-best-place-obtain-customer-feedback

Admin. (2016, February 11). *Celebrity reputation repair: Famous examples of successful fixes.* InternetReputation.com. https://www.internetreputation.com/celebrity-reputation-repair-famous-examples-of-successful-fixes/

Afshar, V. (2015, October 15). *50 important customer experience stats for business leaders.* HuffPost. https://www.huffpost.com/entry/50-important-customer-exp_b_8295772

Afshar, V. (2022, May 19). *How to create a better customer experience.* Salesforce. https://www.salesforce.com/blog/customer-experience/

Bachmann, P., & Danise, A. (2022, August 17). *The convergence of personal wellness and Entrepreneurial success.* Forbes. https://www.forbes.com/sites/forbescoachesc ouncil/2022/08/17/the-convergence-of-personal-wellness-and-entrepreneurial-success/

Baer, J. (2021, March 16). *10 online review statistics you need to know for 2022.* Podium. https://www.podium.com/article/online-review-statistics/

Bain & Company. (2015, April 8). *Are you experienced?* https://www.bain.com/insights/are-you-experienced-infographic/

Banfield, T. (n.d.). *14 motivational customer satisfaction quotes.* SurveyMonkey. https://www.getfeedback.com/resources/cx/1 4-motivational-customer-satisfaction-quotes/

Barloso, K. (2020, April 8). *Why timely responses are important to your Google reviews*. Rize Reviews. https://rizereviews.com/why-its-important-to-respond-to-online-reviews-in-a-timely-manner/

Barry. (2019, April 24). *Employee wellbeing is key to business success*. The Fruit People. https://www.thefruitpeople.ie/employee-wellbeing-key-business-success/

Bartsite. (2021, November 19). *5 tips to empower your employees to help get reviews*. Odd Dog. https://odd.dog/local-seo/5-tips-to-empower-your-employees-to-help-get-reviews/

Bassig, M. (2020, August 25). *Customer experience quotes to inspire your team*. ReviewTrackers. https://www.reviewtrackers.com/blog/customer-experience-quotes/

Bassig, M. (2021a, April 28). *Facebook reputation management: Best practices guide for brands*. ReviewTrackers. https://www.reviewtrackers.com/blog/facebook-reputation-management/

Bassig, M. (2021b, October 20). *5 Google Maps Pack strategies to help you rank*. ReviewTrackers. https://www.reviewtrackers.com/blog/google-maps-pack/

Bassig, M. (2022, February 2). *Everything you need to know about Facebook reviews.* ReviewTrackers. https://www.reviewtrackers.com/blog/faceboo k-reviews/

Birkett, A. (2021, June 3). *How to measure customer satisfaction in 8 simple steps.* HubSpot Blog. https://blog.hubspot.com/service/how-to-measure-customer-satisfaction

Bonelli, S. (2022, February 4). *Google reviews: The complete guide for businesses.* Search Engine Journal. https://www.searchenginejournal.com/google-business-profile-reviews/434849/#close

Brainy Quote. (n.d.). *Nikita Khrushchev.* https://www.brainyquote.com/quotes/nikita_k hrushchev_126015

Brooke, C. (2022, July 1). *What these 4 celebrities can teach us about reputation management.* Business 2 Community. https://www.business2community.com/strateg y/4-celebrities-can-teach-us-reputation-management-01450912

Business.gov.au. (2023, March 7). *Social media for business.* https://business.gov.au/online/social-media-for-business

Campbell, C. (2017, April 15). *New study highlights the importance of online reviews in local search.* Social Media Today. https://www.socialmediatoday.com/marketing/new-study-highlights-importance-online-reviews-local-search

Chan, J. (2023, February 21). *Online reviews: How to use them to your brand's advantage.* Mention. https://mention.com/en/blog/leverage-online-reviews/

Choksi, S. (2017, August 16). *Customer service beats omnichannel perfection, CMO Council study reveals.* LinkedIn. https://www.linkedin.com/pulse/customer-service-beats-omnichannel-perfection-cmo-council-choksi/

Clark, H. (2023, June 8). *12 best customer review management software in 2023.* The CX Lead. https://thecxlead.com/tools/best-customer-review-management-software/

Collier, M. (2011, March 24). *New research proves that responding to negative feedback online benefits companies.* MackCollier.com. http://mackcollier.com/study-responding-to-negative/

Courvoisier, K. (2019, February 22). *Use Google reviews to drive traffic to your new location.* Thanx. https://www.thanx.com/using-google-reviews-drive-traffic-new-location/

Das, R. (2023, March 16). *12 smart ways to ask for a review [+templates].* Statusbrew. https://statusbrew.com/insights/how-to-ask-for-a-review/#how-to-ask-for-a-review-on-review-sites

DataReportal. (2023, May 9). *Digital 2022 global overview report (January 2022) v05.* SlideShare. https://www.slideshare.net/datareportal/digital-2022-global-overview-report-january-2022-v05

Deshpande, H. (n.d.). *Consistency: The winning idea to customer satisfaction.* QuestionPro. https://www.questionpro.com/blog/consistency-the-winning-idea-to-customer-satisfaction/

Diaz, M. (n.d.). *The psychology of reviews (and why to analyze them).* Keatext. https://www.keatext.ai/en/blog/online-reviews/the-psychology-behind-ratings-and-reviews/

Donahue, M. (2018, April 18). *Location3 case study.* Location3. https://www.location3.com/wp-

content/uploads/2018/04/Location3-case-
study_PPC-Reviews-Correlation-2018.pdf

Dublino, J. (2023, March 28). *Smart ways to use customer
feedback.* Business.com.
https://www.business.com/articles/how-to-
use-customer-feedback/

Editor's Choice, (2023, January 11). *4 causes of unhappy
employees and how to deal with them.* Hppy.
https://gethppy.com/workplace-happiness/4-
causes-of-unhappiness-in-the-workplace-and-
how-to-deal-with-them

Enberg, J. (2021, January 12). *Why small businesses could
benefit from the launch of Facebook shops.* Insider
Intelligence.
https://www.insiderintelligence.com/content/
why-small-businesses-could-benefit-launch-of-
facebook-shops

Forsey, C. (2023, February 21). *Reputation Management:
How to protect your brand online in 2023.* HubSpot
Blog.
https://blog.hubspot.com/marketing/reputatio
n-management

Fox, A., Blackman, A., Hanson, E., Slovic, J., & Martin,
R. (2019, March 22). *Research: The experience impact,
according to consumers.* Merkle.
https://www.merkle.com/thought-

leadership/white-papers/experience-impact

Frichou, F. (2022, July 8). *Social proof: What is it, and why is it important for ecommerce?* Trustpilot. https://business.trustpilot.com/reviews/build-trusted-brand/what-is-social-proof-and-why-is-it-important-for-marketing

G5. (2020, August 18). *Reputation management: Tips and templates to respond to reviews like a pro.* https://www.getg5.com/reputation-management-tips-and-templates-for-online-review-response/

Gaffney, A. (2020, August 7). *Consumer surveys confirm: Covid-19 shaking traditional retailer and brand loyalties.* Retail TouchPoints. https://www.retailtouchpoints.com/topics/loyalty/consumer-surveys-confirm-covid-19-shaking-traditional-retailer-and-brand-loyalties

Gallo, A. (2014, October 29). *The value of keeping the right customers.* Harvard Business Review. https://hbr.org/2014/10/the-value-of-keeping-the-right-customers

Gilliam, E. (2022, March 30). *Best customer feedback tools in 2022.* Mopinion. https://mopinion.com/customer-feedback-tools/

Glance. (2022, February 22). *10 ways to exceed expectations in customer service.* https://ww2.glance.net/blog/10-ways-to-exceed-expectations-in-customer-service/

Goodreads. (n.d.). *Quote by Marilyn Suttle.* https://www.goodreads.com/quotes/273216-thank-your-customer-for-complaining-and-mean-it-most-will

Hartshorne, D. (2022, October 27). *5 ways to turn customer feedback into amazing social media posts.* Sendible. https://www.sendible.com/insights/customer-feedback-on-social-media

Hellebuyck, M., Nguyen, T., Halphern, M., Fritze, D., & Kennedy, J. (2017, May 2). *Mind the workplace.* Mental Health America. https://mhanational.org/sites/default/files/Mind%20the%20Workplace%20-%20MHA%20Workplace%20Health%20Survey%202017%20FINAL.PDF

Hennessey, J. (2022, September 19). *Google Local Pack: What is it?* Search Engine Journal. https://www.searchenginejournal.com/google-local-pack/463476/#close

Herrity, J. (2023, February 3). *The importance of job security in the workplace (with tips)*. Indeed. https://www.indeed.com/career-advice/career-development/job-security

Hollingsworth, S. (2023, April 29). *7 reasons why content needs amazing images, videos & visuals*. Search Engine Journal. https://www.searchenginejournal.com/why-content-needs-amazing-images-videos-visuals/268911/

Hore, P. (2022, June 23). *5 must-read social media success stories in 2023*. WP Social Ninja. https://wpsocialninja.com/5-must-read-social-media-success-story-in-2022/

InMoment. (n.d.). *Earning (and destroying) customer loyalty: Retail CX trends you need to know*. https://inmoment.com/blog/earning-and-destroying-customer-loyalty-retail-cx-trends-you-need-to-know/

Jovancic, N. (2020, May 5). *"How did you hear about us?" Survey (Options + Template)*. LeadQuizzes. https://www.leadquizzes.com/blog/how-did-you-hear-about-us/

Kerridge Commercial Systems. (n.d.). *10 inspirational tech quotes*. https://blog.kerridgecs.com/10-

inspirational-tech-quotes

Kimp. (2021, August 9). *6 creative ways to share customer reviews on social.* https://www.kimp.io/customer-reviews/

Knight, R. (2017, December 26). *What to do when you don't feel valued at work.* Harvard Business Review. https://hbr.org/2017/12/what-to-do-when-you-dont-feel-valued-at-work

Leggett, K. (2018, January 24). *2018 customer service trends: How operations become faster and cheaper and yet more human.* Forrester. https://www.forrester.com/report/2018-Customer-Service-Trends-How-Operations-Become-Faster-Cheaper-And-Yet-More-Human/RES142291

Lew, M. (2022, February 15). *Business owner wellbeing: The key to growth.* SME News. https://www.sme-news.co.uk/business-owner-wellbeing-the-key-to-growth/

Luca, M. (2016, March). *Reviews, reputation, and revenue: The case of Yelp.com.* Harvard Business School. https://www.hbs.edu/ris/Publication%20Files/12-016_a7e4a5a2-03f9-490d-b093-8f951238dba2.pdf

Lyubomirsky, S., Boehm, J. K., & Walsh, L. C. (2018,

August 15). *The relationship between happiness and career success isn't as clear as you might think*. The World Economic Forum. https://www.weforum.org/agenda/2018/08/is-happiness-a-consequence-or-cause-of-career-success

MacDonald, S. (2023, March 16). *Customer service benchmark report (new for 2023)*. SuperOffice CRM. https://www.superoffice.com/blog/customer-service-benchmark-report/

Marchant, R. (2017, March 15). *How do online reviews impact businesses? find out pros and cons*. BrightLocal. https://www.brightlocal.com/blog/the-impact-of-online-reviews/

Markey, R. (n.d.). *Are you undervaluing your customers?* Harvard Business Review. https://hbr.org/2020/01/are-you-undervaluing-your-customers

Martinez, N. (2023, April 8). *155 Balance quotes on life and peace of mind (2023)*. Everyday Power. https://everydaypower.com/balance-quotes/

McCain, A. (2023, January 16). *28 critical customer retention statistics [2023]: Average customer retention rate by industry*. Zippia. https://www.zippia.com/advice/customer-retention-statistics/

McCarthy, C. (2010, March 19). *Nestle mess shows sticky side of Facebook pages.* CNET. https://www.cnet.com/culture/nestle-mess-shows-sticky-side-of-facebook-pages/

McCormick, K. (2023, March 28). *How to ask for reviews (with examples & templates!).* WordStream. https://www.wordstream.com/blog/ws/2020/07/16/how-to-ask-for-reviews

Mershon, P. (2012, January 18). *9 Small business social media success stories.* Social Media Examiner. https://www.socialmediaexaminer.com/9-small-business-social-media-success-stories/

Mobilesquared. (2010, June). *Conversational advertising.* https://mobilesquared.co.uk/wp-content/uploads/2017/12/Conversational-Advertising.pdf

Monae, A. (2022, July 20). *Why You need to prioritize your health over your business.* Entrepreneur. https://www.entrepreneur.com/living/why-you-need-to-prioritize-your-health-over-your-business/431435

Nayak, N., Tweten, C., Constantine, L., Dawer, N., & Haynes, A. (2020, November 11). *52 customer satisfaction quotes to inspire you to start measuring customer satisfaction now.* Zonka Feedback. https://www.zonkafeedback.com/blog/custom er-satisfaction-quotes

Nelson, L. (2021, March 4). *How to ask customers to remove negative feedback in 2023.* Signpost. https://www.signpost.com/blog/ask-customers-remove-negative-feedback-templates/

Novik, O. (2021, August 16). *10 outstanding principles of managing and exceeding customers expectations.* WOW24-7. https://wow24-7.io/blog/10-principles-of-managing-and-exceeding-customers-expectations

OmegaTheme. (2020, July 16). *The psychology behind online ratings and reviews.* https://www.omegatheme.com/blog/101-facebook-reviews/334-the-psychology-behind-reviews-and-ratings-of-online-users

Oswald, A. J. (2015). *Happiness and productivity.* Warwick WRAP. https://wrap.warwick.ac.uk/63228/7/WRAP_Oswald_681096.pdf

Paget, S. (2023, February 7). *Local consumer review survey 2023: Customer reviews and behavior.* BrightLocal. https://www.brightlocal.com/research/local-consumer-review-survey/

Pencak, S. (n.d.). *Top 50 social media quotes | Inspiration.* Silvia Pencak. https://silviapencak.com/top-50-social-media-quotes/

Perzynska, K., & Fox, S. (2023, May 15). *How did you hear about us survey—What it is and why you need one.* Survicate. https://survicate.com/surveys/how-did-you-hear-about-us/

Pinkham, R. (2022, August 30). *5 ways to see how new customers are finding your business.* Constant Contact. https://www.constantcontact.com/blog/how-customers-find-business/

Podium. (2017). *Podium 2017 state of online reviews.* https://learn.podium.com/rs/841-BRM-380/images/Podium-2017-State-of-Online-Reviews.pdf

PowerReviews. (2021, May 19). *Survey: The ever-growing power of reviews.* https://www.powerreviews.com/insights/power-of-reviews-survey-2021/

Proserpio, D., & Zervas, G. (2018, February 14). *Study: Replying to customer reviews results in better ratings.* Harvard Business Review. https://hbr.org/2018/02/study-replying-to-customer-reviews-results-in-better-ratings

Qualtrics. (n.d.). *Your guide to measuring customer satisfaction.* https://www.qualtrics.com/au/experience-management/customer/measure-customer-satisfaction/

Redbord, M. (2022, June 24). *The hard truth about acquisition costs (and how your customers can save you).* HubSpot Blog. https://blog.hubspot.com/service/customer-acquisition-study

Reputation. (n.d.). *MedQuest increases patient acquisition and retention through improved review responding.* https://reputation.com/resources/customer-stories/medquest-increases-patient-acquisition-and-retention-through-improved-review-responding/

ReviewTrackers. (2021, May 24). *Asking for reviews from customers: The ultimate guide.* https://www.reviewtrackers.com/guides/ask-customers-review/

ReviewTrackers. (2022a, January 9). *2022 Report: Online reviews statistics and trends.* https://www.reviewtrackers.com/reports/online-reviews-survey/

ReviewTrackers. (2022b, February 16). *Powerful examples*

of how to respond to negative reviews. https://www.reviewtrackers.com/guides/exam ples-responding-reviews/

Richardson, B. (2022, December 5). *Employee statistics & facts - 2022 research by acuity training!* Acuity Training. https://www.acuitytraining.co.uk/news-tips/employee-happiness-statistics-facts/

RightNow Technologies. (2012, January 11). *2011 customer experience impact report.* SlideShare. https://www.slideshare.net/RightNow/2011-customer-experience-impact-report#5

RingCentral Team. (2020, March 1). *Meeting & exceeding customer expectations: an in-depth guide.* RingCentral. https://www.ringcentral.com/us/en/blog/cust omer-expectations/

Rise. (2018, April 24). *12 inspiring quotes to help small business owners.* https://risepeople.com/blog/quotes-for-small-business-owners/

Schooley, S. (2023, March 27). *Why happy employees are good for business.* Business.com. https://www.business.com/articles/a-good-investment-how-keeping-employees-happy-benefits-a-business/

Shibu, S. (2020, September 2). *Businesses, take note: Your customers prefer texts.* PCMag. https://www.pcmag.com/news/businesses-take-note-your-customers-prefer-texts

Shrestha, K., Hawkinson, J., Dy, L., & Messier, S. (2022, December 2). *50 online reviews stats for 2022 [Infographic].* Vendasta. https://www.vendasta.com/blog/50-stats-you-need-to-know-about-online-reviews/

Sickler, J. (2022, March 3). *Why online reviews are important for customers & businesses.* Terakeet. https://terakeet.com/blog/online-reviews/

Smith, A. (2021, August 4). *How the right incentive can help you generate more reviews.* PowerReviews. https://www.powerreviews.com/blog/what-incentives-generate-reviews/

Sprague, D. (2021, August 25). *Ecommerce 'psychology of product reviews' survey 2021.* Shopper Approved. https://results.shopperapproved.com/blog/eco mmerce-psychology-of-product-reviews-survey-2021

Stanley, H. (2021, March 25). *How to use customer reviews to improve your business.* GatherUp. https://gatherup.com/blog/use-customer-reviews-to-improve-your-business/

Stattin, N. (2023, February 24). *32 customer experience statistics you need to know for 2023.* SuperOffice CRM. https://www.superoffice.com/blog/customer-experience-statistics/

The Restaurant Boss. (n.d.). *"A satisfied customer is the best business strategy of all." -Michael LeBoeuf.* https://therestaurantboss.com/leboeuf-satisfied-customer/

Tiwari, K. (2022, May 19). *6 customer satisfaction metrics to start measuring.* Zapier. https://zapier.com/blog/customer-satisfaction-metrics/

Tolliver-Walker, H. (2020, June 3). *Got emotional connection? Then you've got profits.* WhatTheyThink. https://whattheythink.com/articles/101071-got-emotional-connection-then-youve-got-profits/

Upvoty. (n.d.). *5 things you can do to simplify user feedback.* https://www.upvoty.com/5-things-you-can-do-to-simplify-user-feedback/

Walker. (n.d.). *Customers 2020: A progress report.* https://walkerinfo.com/cxleader/customers-

2020-a-progress-report/

Widewail Team. (n.d.). *Google reviews: How to respond to positive & negative reviews.* Widewail. https://www.widewail.com/guide-review-response#chapter8

Willas, S. (2023, April 4). *7 reasons why online reviews are essential for your brand.* Mention. https://mention.com/en/blog/online-reviews/

WOMMA. (2014, November 18). *Landmark study shows word of mouth drives 13% of consumer sales.* PR Newswire. https://www.prnewswire.com/news-releases/landmark-study-shows-word-of-mouth-drives-13-of-consumer-sales-283040971.html

Woods, A. (2023, May 9). *Four ideas for sharing your client testimonials on social media.* https://www.linkedin.com/pulse/four-ideas-sharing-your-client-testimonials-social-media-amy-woods/

Made in the USA
Middletown, DE
16 September 2024

60484047R00150